HOW TO FEED AN ARMY:
RECIPES AND LORE FROM THE FRONT LINES

J. G. LEWIN & P. J. HUFF

HOW TO FEED AN ARMY:
RECIPES AND LORE FROM THE FRONT LINES

J. G. LEWIN & P. J. HUFF

Collins

An Imprint of HarperCollins*Publishers*

To Airman First Class R.L. Huff and Private First Class D.H. Lewin, both of whom were well fed in service to their country during World War II and the Korean Conflict, and who had the great good fortune to marry the women who really taught us how to feed an army.

—J.G.L. & P.J.H.

Produced for HarperCollins by:

Hydra Publishing
129 Main Street
Irvington, NY 10533
www.hylaspublishing.com

FIRST EDITION

The name of the "Smithsonian," "Smithsonian Institution," and the sunburst logo are registered trademarks of the Smithsonian Institution.

Library of Congress Cataloging-in-Publication Data

ISBN-10: 0-06-089111-4
ISBN-13: 978-0-06-089111-4

06 07 08 09 10 IM 10 9 8 7 6 5 4 3 2 1

TITLE PAGE: World War II flight nurses take a break for chow soon after arriving to pick up wounded at an airstrip near the fighting front in Burma in 1944.

CONTENTS

"—THEN WE'D USE 860 EGGS—!"

FOREWORD

NEAR BURNSIDE'S BRIDGE ON THE ANTIETAM
National Battlefield stands a historical marker commemorating the service of a Union commissary sergeant. As the Twenty-third Ohio Infantry held the line near the bridge on that long and sultry day in September 1862, Commissary Sergeant William McKinley set to work bringing hot coffee and roast beef to the front line. In the course of the battle, McKinley made several trips to the front despite having his first team of mules killed by shrapnel as he moved forward. Exposing himself to enemy shot and shell, he brought food and drink to his hungry and thirsty comrades and earned their admiration and respect. The world knows of Sergeant McKinley's services because he later became president of the United States.

Commissary Sergeant William McKinley, circa 1862. (Courtesy West Virginia State Archives.)

For more than 225 years, untold numbers of others have worked tirelessly, often unheralded, to meet the challenge of keeping U.S. military personnel fed and operating at peak efficiency. Feeding large numbers of troops, often at great distances from their home bases, is extremely difficult. Not only must those responsible for feeding them procure and deliver the necessary foodstuffs, but nutritional needs must be met, waste minimized, and frequent shortages of raw materials dealt with—often in rough operating conditions. All the while, there is the challenge of presenting appetizing meals that the troops will eat day after day.

Soldiers complain about few things more than army chow. Still, they often sing the praises of their company cooks, who could work miracles from a pile of cans and a few fresh ingredients. Cooking for an army is an inherently difficult business, and while failure often produces vociferous complaint, success tends to evoke only the sound of contented chewing and the occasional loud belch. The recipes celebrated in this book may in some small way help redress that imbalance. These recipes epitomize the hard work and ingenuity of the Army cook and soldier (and their comrades in the other services) through the centuries.

From hardtack during the American Revolution and Civil War, to SPAM and C-rations during World War II, to the current Meals Ready-To-Eat (MREs), the U.S. military has worked continuously to improve the quality of Army field rations. And while cooks in the field, and in mess halls and galleys, worked to make the best meals possible—sometimes with some less-than-appetizing ingredients—soldiers, sailors, and airmen used their own ingenuity to take what they received and make it better. The recipes here result from the efforts and devotion of all those involved in perfecting these dishes. If you need to cook for a crowd, you can certainly benefit from the wisdom found here, distilled from the experiences of hundreds of thousands of military cooks preparing many billions of meals.

Clifford J. Rogers   Steve R. Waddell
Department of History, United States Military Academy

INTRODUCTION

FOR A PERIOD SOMEWHAT LONGER THAN WE HAVE HAD A
country, we have had a military. And, while tactics, training, weapons, and logistics have changed, there are some things that don't change. The troops patrolling Baghdad have some fundamental characteristics in common with the Minutemen who answered the call to Lexington and Concord.

To a man (or woman, nowadays), a universal question has been on the lips of our troops since Paul Revere took his momentous ride: What's for chow? From the day Thomas Mifflin took over as the first quartermaster general in August 1775, the military has been doing its level best to figure out how to feed an army. It has been no easy task.

Problems of logistics. Dangers in the field. Shifting standards of quality. Changing tastes. An evolving sense of what constitutes "healthy" (you just don't see much suet or lard in mess halls anymore). Campaigns ranging from the parched earth of the Mexican War to the mud of the Civil War to the Arctic of World War II to the rain forests of Vietnam to the heat of Iraq.

The line that passes through the earliest gill of rum served on Breed's Hill overlooking Boston and runs through an MRE in Kuwait is far from straight. It has veered over the years in some rather surprising directions. In this volume we do not attempt to document the full range of the military's culinary wanderings. Rather we have attempted to provide a flavor, if you will, of the recipes that have been employed over the years to feed our troops in the field.

Each recipe is authentic and has been gleaned from primary sources and official military cookbooks. We have attempted to keep the ingredients, proportions, and directions as close to the original as is possible. You are given the same directions that were given to military cooks serving in the trenches or in the desert. Following these recipes to the letter, you would be able to feed an army of a hundred troopers.

Troops stationed in England during World War II serve themselves but are told not to waste anything.

We then modified each recipe, changing proportions, and—in some few cases—updating ingredients so that it may be prepared in a contemporary kitchen for a much smaller contingent of the home militia.

Along the way, we've added some spice in the form of slang, military lore, and a few tall tales that shed some light on the traditions of military cookery . . . the high points and the low points, the successes and the absurdities.

This is one-part cookbook. It is also one-part history book. And it has been compiled with respect for the men and women who have served our country with honor.

—J.G. Lewin & P.J. Huff

Cadets have lunch at the United States Military Academy at West Point.

Colonel George Washington's Small Beer
Banana Milk Drink
Boston Coffee
Cocoa or Chocolate
Fresh Fruit Punch
Spruce Beer

CHAPTER 1
BEVERAGES

COLONEL GEORGE WASHINGTON'S SMALL BEER
AMERICAN REVOLUTION

The father of our country liked his beer. In his younger days he was particularly fond of British porter. As he grew older, however, he wasn't particularly fond of anything British. Luckily there were a number of brewers in America, and he was able to make the transition to domestic ales without a lot of fuss.

Washington was in the habit of keeping meticulous notebooks throughout his life, and nearly all survive in public archives. In 1757, as a colonel in the Virginia militia, he recorded his favorite recipe for small beer.

Small beer is usually the weakest of a brew. It was common fare for the general population in colonial America. This was a time when water was far from pure, and partaking of either brewed or distilled spirits was far healthier than just slipping down to the creek for a quick drink.

One of General Washington's first acts as commander of the Continental Army in the Revolution was to order that all troops should get a quart of beer with their daily ration. Perhaps he used this very recipe.

Be aware, though, if you try this one yourself, it isn't weak. The good colonel's recipe packs about twice the alcohol content of beer sold over the bar today.

ORDERS: Take a large siffer [sifter] full of Bran Hops to your Tast[e] — Boil these 3 hours then strain out 30 Gall[ons] into a cooler put in 3 Gall[ons] Molasses while the Beer is Scalding hot or rather draw the Melasses into the cooler & st[r]ain the Beer on it while boiling Hot. Let this stand till it is little more than Blood warm then put in a quart of Yea[s]t if the Weather is very cold cover it over with a Blank[et] & let it Work in the Cooler 24 hours then put it into the Cask — leave the bung open till it is almost don[e] Working — Bottle it that day Week it was brewed.

SLANG

Liquor
Civil War: bark juice, anti-fragmatic, booze, bug juice, joy juice, nokum stiff, oh-be-joyful, old red-eye, popskull, tar water
World War I: skee, zig-zag
World War II: bamboo juice, hard soup, tarantula soup, serum, strike-me-dead

BANANA MILK DRINK
VIETNAM WAR

Banana milk is a drink popular throughout Asia. It actually became a bit of a craze in South Korea during the 1970s, where it was reported to be the best-selling item in convenience stores (beating cigarettes, soda, and candy bars).

This recipe was used by the military during the Vietnam War.

FOR AN ARMY OF 100

RATIONS: 5 gallons water
5 pounds nonfat
dry milk
15 eggs, beaten
$^3/_4$ tablespoon salt
2 $^1/_4$ cups sugar
4 tablespoons vanilla
4 quarts mashed
bananas

FOR AN ARMY OF 10

RATIONS: 1 $^1/_2$ quarts water
1 $^1/_2$ cups nonfat
dry milk
2 eggs, beaten
Dash salt
$^1/_3$ cup sugar
1 teaspoon vanilla
1 $^1/_2$ cups mashed
bananas

ORDERS: Sprinkle dry milk on the surface of the water; beat with a whisk just enough to blend milk and water. Stir in eggs, salt, sugar, and vanilla. Add bananas and blend thoroughly. Chill before serving.

Vietnam War era. Preparing salad in a well-appointed base kitchen.

BOSTON COFFEE
KOREAN WAR

This variation on a basic cup of joe popped up in the recipe book published jointly by the Army and the Air Force in November 1950, and then it disappeared.

The instructions warn: "This may not be popular." Maybe it would be best to serve it with creamed chipped beef so all the griping could be gotten over with at once.

FOR AN ARMY OF 100

RATIONS: 3 $\frac{1}{2}$ gallons coffee
1 $\frac{1}{2}$ gallons evaporated milk
1 $\frac{1}{2}$ gallons water

FOR AN ARMY OF 10

RATIONS: 5 cups coffee
2 $\frac{3}{4}$ cups evaporated milk
2 $\frac{3}{4}$ cups water

ORDERS: Use half recipe for coffee and prepare coffee. Scald 1 1/2 gallons of evaporated milk with 1 1/2 gallons water and mix with prepared coffee. Serve hot. This may not be popular. Learn whether the men in your mess like it before preparing it.

Summer in Korea. On a balmy June day in 1951, GIs line up for chow in Kunsan during "World War II-and-a-half" (as they sometimes called the Korean War).

COCOA OR CHOCOLATE
WORLD WAR I

Hot cocoa has long been an acceptable substitute for coffee. In the days of sailing ships it was more common than coffee.

During World War II, chocolate was packed into K-rations for the troops in the field, along with directions for making hot cocoa from the bar. The *Technical Manual for the Army Cook*, distributed during World War II, suggests serving this cold during the summer months. This recipe dates to the Army's World War I manual and is just as good as any we've seen.

FOR A SQUAD OF 10

RATIONS: 3 to 5 ounces cocoa
or chocolate
5 ounces sugar
4 ounces evaporated milk
1 gallon (scant) of water

FOR A DETAIL OF 5

RATIONS: 1 $\frac{1}{2}$ to 3 $\frac{1}{2}$ ounces chocolate or
6 $\frac{1}{2}$ tablespoons to 1 cup cocoa
$\frac{1}{3}$ cup sugar
2 ounces evaporated milk
8 cups water

ORDERS: Bring water to a boil, add cocoa, and boil 5 minutes; add milk and sugar to taste. Whip slightly with a wire whipper before serving. Serve hot.

"This ham doesn't taste right," said the rookie.

"The cook said it was cured last week," said the Vet.

"Huh! Take it from me, it must have had a relapse then."

—Sergeant Major Edward D. Rose in *Khaki Komedy* (1918)

FOR COFFEE AND COUNTRY

The American military's love affair with coffee has been a long-standing and beautiful thing.

It started back in the days of the Revolution. Seems there had been this tea party up in Boston, and it became suddenly unpatriotic to drink tea. Congress even said so, deciding that coffee should be the national beverage and mandating it on ships of the fledging Navy. So we switched to coffee and never really looked back.

Even though Congress directed that coffee be served at sea, it made no provision for mandating it for the Army. Coffee was not part of the standard daily ration approved by Congress for those serving during either the Revolutionary War or the War of 1812 (whiskey, rum, and brandy were, however). Coffee finally made its way to the approved daily rations during the Mexican War, when each man was allotted about an ounce a day. (Official rations of distilled spirits were taken away from the Army at that point; in the Navy they would continue until officially banned in 1914.)

The coffee allotment increased significantly during the Civil War, to about 1 3/4 ounces per man per day. And that was the

Instant cream for coffee

case for both sides. Of course, what was allotted and what was actually received were two different things.

Coffee was a Federal-blockaded item during the Civil War, and far more precious than cotton in the South. As the war progressed, only rarely did the Confederate soldier see coffee, and then only when he found a way of getting it from his Federal foe. One of the more common ways of doing so would be to establish an informal truce along the picket lines. Johnny Reb would trade his plug of tobacco to Billy Yank for a ration of coffee. (They'd also trade newspapers, lies, and insults. Not a bad way to pass the time between pitched battles.)

Stories abound of coffee innovation amid deprivation in the South during the war. Newspapers would print recipes for coffee substitutes (burnt sugar, parched rye, chinquapin nuts, acorns, and various mixtures of corn meal), and belles would write letters extolling the virtues of one form or another for entertaining.

When, just prior to World War I, distilled spirits were banned from all naval depots and vessels by Secretary of the Navy Josephus Daniels, coffee began to come into its own in the Navy.

There is a story, probably not quite true, that coffee made a significant contribution to naval attire. There had been a dust-up in 1914 involving naval personnel on an island just off Mexico. We won't go into detail, but suffice it to say some Americans wound up in jail (but you shouldda seen the other guys!). Anyway, the Marines, accompanied by a party of sailors, were going in to get them out. Problem was, the sailors had no appropriate attire, since their kit consisted of either blue woolens or dress whites, neither of which was deemed suitable for combat on a tropical shore. The problem was solved by an enterprising cook on a destroyer who dipped the whites into vats of coffee, thereby creating the first khakis. Well, maybe . . . it could've happened.

Coffee became a rationed item on the home front for a period during World War II, not because there was a shortage of beans, but because there was a shortage of ships to move the beans. It appears they were tied up in other endeavors (like running supplies to Europe). That problem didn't last long, though. Early in the war Washington set up a barge line to run coffee and sugar from Cuba to Florida. Good thing, too, because coffee consumption had risen to a record fifteen pounds per capita in 1944.

With the advent of C-rations and K-rations at the onset of World War II, coffee came to the front lines in neat little pouches that could be easily warmed in a foxhole. (At least they said it was coffee.) The Army's new canteens even came complete with a form-fitting metal coffee mug. The daily allotment had climbed to two ounces per man per day. But it was the Navy that really got serious about its coffee during World War II. Early in the morning on the day after the attack on Pearl Harbor, undamaged and lightly damaged ships put to sea. But before they left, they took on five tons of coffee. This was due to the efforts of one lieutenant, junior grade, who spent the afternoon of December 7, 1941, running all over the islands buying every bean he could find.

The Navy went so far as to organize and run its own coffee-roasting plants during the war. It actually had three of them, one each in Honolulu, Brooklyn, and Oakland, California. Each could roast 500 pounds of green beans every fifteen minutes.

Navy coffee is legendary. There are those who will tell you that the Pacific fleet ran on caffeine rather than fuel oil. That may be stretching a point, but not by a whole lot. Coffeepots were everywhere on board ship. If you could find an electrical outlet, chances are you'd find a pot. Some of it (most of it?) was just awful. But it was hot. And it was certainly coffeelike. It did its job for Victory.

Union soldiers cooking in camp during the Civil War

All Hands magazine, a monthly publication of the U.S. Navy, reported on an extraordinary rig in its August 1949 issue:

> Probably the most complicated joe pot ever used in the Navy was one rigged in the engine room of a wartime transport. Designed and built through the combined efforts of several engineering, construction and coffee-brewing "experts," it was a Rube Goldbergish–looking affair with a half a dozen pressure valves, vacuum lines, drain lines, safety valves and water and coffee level indicators. The "pot" would boil on either hot or exhaust steam through an arrangement that put a vacuum drag on it when desired. Procuring a cup of joe was more complicated than operating the main engines, and no one under a first-class petty officer was allowed to touch it. Sailors who once tasted beverages brewed in this contraption say all other coffee is flat and tasteless in comparison.

If you pulled K.P. duty, you'd get in big trouble if you ever scoured the metal coffeepot. Never do that. You can rinse it, but you do not scour because that will remove the backlog of good coffee oil that has built up on the walls of the pot. And it takes a long time to build up that oil.

These days coffee bars are commonplace in military installations around the world. Maybe the stuff is a little fancier now, what with lattes and cappuccinos and espressos. But you can still get a good, strong black cup of joe. And you will still find a pouch of instant coffee in your MRE.

And the chances are good that if you can find an outlet, you will still find a pot with something that passes for coffee.

FRESH FRUIT PUNCH
KOREAN WAR

Fresh fruits and vegetables for troops in the field were rare prior to the Korean War. But advances in refrigerated shipping methods and the use of portable refrigerated boxes in the field made available a variety of fresh fruits and vegetables for the combat troops.

To ward off the summer heat and to provide necessary vitamins, this refreshing blend of juice and fruit was served to the troops in Korea.

FOR AN ARMY OF 100

RATIONS: 8 $\frac{1}{2}$ pounds
granulated sugar
1 $\frac{1}{2}$ gallons hot water
4 $\frac{1}{2}$ gallons cold
water
1 quart grape juice
40 oranges
30 lemons
8 grapefruit

FOR AN ARMY OF 10

RATIONS: 1 $\frac{1}{2}$ cups granulated
sugar
2 $\frac{1}{2}$ cups hot water
6 cups cold water
$\frac{1}{3}$ cup grape juice
4 oranges
3 lemons
1 grapefruit

ORDERS: Dissolve sugar in hot water. Extract juice from oranges, lemons, and grapefruits. Add cooled sugar syrup to the juices. Add cold water and ice, if available. Serve very cold.

Winter in Korea. Chicken on the hood of a jeep, deep in February 1951. The field mess gear was unchanged from that issued during World War II.

SPRUCE BEER
AMERICAN REVOLUTION

In 1776 Congress detailed the rations due a Continental soldier and included spruce beer in the mix. Including spruce beer, cider, and molasses, each soldier was to receive nine gallons each week. An important component of this fermented beverage is the essence of spruce, which was made by "decocting" or boiling the shoots and buds of the spruce tree. Today, spruce essence can be purchased from home-brewery supply houses.

In 1796, Amelia Simmons published this recipe for Spruce Beer in her book, *American Cookery*.

> Take four ounces of hops, let them boil half an hour in 1 gallon of water. Strain the hop water, then add 16 gallons warm water, 2 gallons of molasses, 8 ounces of essence of spruce dissolved in 1 quart of water. Put it in a clean cask, then shake well together, add half a pint of emptins, then let stand and work one week; if very warm weather less time will do. When it is drawn off to bottle, add 1 spoonful of molasses to every bottle.

The "emptins" that Ms. Simmons refers to was a type of yeast made from hops and potatoes. It was a common leavening agent in most kitchens of the eighteenth and nineteenth centuries.

The 1863 version of Spruce Beer, published in a Southern newspaper, lists ingredients more familiar to the cooks of our time:

RATIONS: 3 gallons hot water ("blood warmth")
1 $\frac{1}{2}$ half pints molasses
1 tablespoon essence of spruce
1 tablespoon ginger
1 gill ($\frac{1}{2}$ cup) yeast

ORDERS: Combine hot water, molasses, essence of spruce, and ginger. Add the yeast, mixing well. Let stand overnight. Bottle in the morning. "It will be in good condition to drink in twenty-four hours."

Made from a cow's horn, this cup saw duty during the American Revolution. The owner's initials, "WCW," are inscribed on the side.

CHAPTER 2
SOUPS, SALADS & SANDWICHES

PEPPER POT SOUP
VIETNAM WAR

Credit for this creation goes to Christopher Ludwick (1720–1801) of Philadelphia. And while this particular version dates to the Vietnam War, the original made its appearance during the American Revolution.

It was that horrible winter of 1777–78, when General Washington and his army were camped at Valley Forge, just outside the City of Brotherly Love. Things weren't going all that well for our side just then. Washington had been forced to abandon both New York and Philadelphia to British forces. His army, what was left of it, was ill-provisioned. Not enough clothing. Certainly not enough food. These were the days "that try men's souls" to which Thomas Paine referred.

Enter Christopher Ludwick, superintendent of bakers for the Continental Army. Perhaps it was his background of having survived a siege in an earlier European war that gave him the skill to improvise as he did. He was a resourceful man. And at Valley Forge, he decided to make soup.

It was essentially a concoction of whatever he could find, including old potatoes, bits of vegetables, and ill-defined pieces of meat. About the best that could be said for it was that it was hot. So, in order to disguise the taste, he threw in lots of hot red peppers and peppercorns.

It worked. Tradition has it that, following the meal, the troops were so invigorated they called "Bring on the Redcoats!" Whether or not this is true, we can say that the army lived to fight another day. There are those, primarily from Philadelphia, who call this "the soup that won the war." And maybe they're right.

This version of the recipe, first presented during the Vietnam War, does not call for any meat. The spirit of the original lives on, however, in that it is designed to help the cook use whatever ingredients are on hand.

Vinka Kovelenko: "Do you think the colonel would be fooled by such a ridiculous statement?"

Major Chuck Lockwood: "If he'll eat Army food, he'll swallow anything!"

—From the 1956 film *The Iron Petticoat*, starring Katherine Hepburn and Bob Hope

FOR AN ARMY OF 100

RATIONS: 2 cups butter
or margarine
1 $\frac{1}{2}$ cups onions,
dry, chopped
4 $\frac{1}{2}$ cups sweet
peppers, chopped
1 $\frac{1}{2}$ quarts celery,
sliced
2 cups flour, wheat
5 gallons stock,
beef or chicken
6 pounds white
potatoes, chopped
2 teaspoons black
pepper
6 tablespoons salt
2 $\frac{3}{4}$ cups nonfat
dry milk
1 $\frac{1}{2}$ cups warm water
1 cup canned
pimientos, chopped

FOR AN ARMY OF 10

RATIONS: 3 tablespoons butter
$\frac{1}{4}$ cup onion, chopped
$\frac{1}{4}$ cup sweet peppers,
chopped
$\frac{2}{3}$ cup celery, sliced
3 tablespoons flour
7 $\frac{1}{2}$ cups stock,
beef or chicken
1 $\frac{1}{2}$ cups potatoes,
chopped
Pepper to taste
1 $\frac{3}{4}$ teaspoons salt
$\frac{3}{4}$ cup fresh milk
1 tablespoon pimiento

ORDERS: Sauté vegetables in butter or margarine 10 minutes. Do not brown. Remove from fat and set aside. Blend fat and flour together, stirring until smooth. Add cold roux to stock, stirring constantly. Cook until blended. Add sautéed vegetables, potatoes, and seasonings. Cook about 20 minutes, or until vegetables are tender. Reconstitute milk (if necessary). Immediately prior to serving, remove soup from heat, slowly adding milk, stirring constantly. Add pimientos.

CREAM OF MUSHROOM SOUP
VIETNAM WAR

One of the advantages of this recipe for the military cook is that the main ingredients (mushrooms and milk) are canned and are usually right there on the shelf ready to be used.

This hot soup could be whipped up on a cold day when fresh vegetables were running low or depleted. For the family cook, this creamy soup can satisfy the home army on the night before the weekly shopping excursion!

FOR AN ARMY OF 100

RATIONS: 7 pounds mushrooms, canned, chopped, or sliced (14 8-ounce cans)
2 $\frac{1}{4}$ cups onions, dry, chopped
2 pounds butter
2 pounds flour, wheat, hard
6 tablespoons salt
2 teaspoons black pepper
4 gallons chicken stock or water or reserved liquid
2 gallons milk, evaporated (undiluted)

FOR AN ARMY OF 10

RATIONS: 2 6.5-ounce cans mushrooms
$\frac{1}{4}$ cup onions
$\frac{1}{3}$ cup butter or margarine
$\frac{2}{3}$ cup all-purpose flour
1 $\frac{3}{4}$ teaspoons salt
Dash pepper
1 $\frac{1}{2}$ quarts chicken stock and reserved mushroom liquid
3 cups milk, evaporated (undiluted)

ORDERS: Drain mushrooms; reserve liquid. Peel, wash, and chop onions finely. Melt butter in stockpot. Add drained mushrooms and onions; mix well; cook 5 minutes or until onions are a light yellow. Add flour, pepper, and salt, stirring until well mixed. Add chicken stock mixture, stirring constantly. Bring to a boil, reduce heat, simmer 15 minutes. Add milk just before serving, stirring constantly. Heat to serving temperature. DO NOT BOIL.

BAKED BEAN SANDWICHES
VIETNAM WAR

They ate 'em hot and they ate 'em cold. Sometimes, just for a little variety, they put 'em between two slices of bread and ate 'em with their hands. If you like beans, this one is for you.

Beans are a good source of protein and can be substituted for meat. They are also filling and were always on the cook's shelf. A baked bean sandwich could go a long way to filling a hungry soldier's belly on a cold night.

FOR AN ARMY OF 100

RATIONS: 2 gallons canned
baked beans
with pork
3 cups chopped
fresh celery
2 $\frac{2}{3}$ cups chopped
onions
1 cup chopped sweet
cucumber pickles
3 cups chili sauce
200 slices bread
1 quart butter or
margarine

FOR AN ARMY OF 10

RATIONS: 3 cups canned baked
beans with pork
$\frac{1}{4}$ cup chopped fresh
celery
$\frac{1}{3}$ cup chopped
onions
1 $\frac{1}{2}$ tablespoons
chopped sweet
cucumber pickles
$\frac{1}{4}$ cup chili sauce
20 slices bread
$\frac{1}{3}$ cup butter or
margarine

ORDERS: Drain beans and discard liquid. Mash beans. Combine beans with remaining ingredients; mix thoroughly. Spread bread with butter or margarine. Spread slices of bread with 1/3 cup filling each; top with second slices of bread.

BARLEY SOUP
WORLD WAR I

Breads and soups have been made from barley for about 10,000 years. Romans in Britain are known to have made barley soup, and the Roman gladiators were known as *hordearii*, which means "eaters of barley."

Barley has been a medicinal grain in addition to a staple of human diet. At various times, barley water has been given people of all ages to cure bladder and urinary diseases, hemorrhoids, kidney stones, tumors, and jaundice. It has been added to milk for sickly infants and children and used as a bath for skin irritations and as a cure for pimples.

No doubt our soldiers during World War I had all the benefits of barley when this soup was served

FOR AN ARMY OF 60
RATIONS: 6 gallons beef stock
3 pounds barley
10 pounds tomatoes
1 pound diced bacon

FOR AN ARMY OF 6
RATIONS: 8 cups beef stock
$^2/_3$ cup barley
1 $^1/_2$ cups tomatoes
$^1/_4$ cup diced bacon

ORDERS: Mix all ingredients well, salt and pepper to taste, and allow to boil for 1 hour. If fresh tomatoes are used, they should be stewed and pressed through a colander before being added to the soup. Regulate the amount of beef stock so that when the soup is ready to serve there should be about 6 gallons (10 cups).

This now extremely rare chevron was worn by a cook-private first class in the Great Depression's Civilian Conservation Corps. While not technically part of the military, CCC members did walk, look, and quack like they were.

CABBAGE AND SWEET PEPPER SALAD
VIETNAM WAR

Cabbage keeps well and is rich in vitamin C. Its shelf life makes it a good staple for the military cook.

A quick side dish, this salad is a nice accompaniment to pork or ham. It does equally well as a picnic dish or on a buffet. Try using a mixture of green, yellow, orange, and red peppers in this salad for a colorful addition to your table.

FOR AN ARMY OF 100

RATIONS: 18 pounds shredded cabbage
5 pounds sweet peppers, finely chopped
3 cups French dressing
1 teaspoon black pepper
6 tablespoons salt
1 cup sugar

FOR AN ARMY OF 10

RATIONS: 9 cups shredded cabbage
1 $\frac{1}{2}$ cups sweet peppers, finely chopped
$\frac{1}{4}$ cup French dressing
Dash pepper
1 $\frac{3}{4}$ teaspoons salt
1 $\frac{1}{2}$ tablespoons sugar

ORDERS: Toss cabbage and peppers together lightly. Combine the rest of the ingredients; mix thoroughly. Pour dressing over cabbage mixture; toss lightly. Allow to stand 15 minutes before serving.

Take all you want, but eat all you take.
—Donald H. Lewin (my dad) addressing his four sons over the dinner table, while thinking back to other mess halls during his service in Word War II. Circa 1963, 1964, 1965, 1966... and continuing.

Donald H. Lewin, with K-rations in the field, during World War II

CANADIAN CHEESE SOUP
VIETNAM WAR

There was a serious movement (well, semi-serious) to change the motto on Wisconsin's license plates to "Eat Cheese or Die." It didn't work, of course. But, hey, it was the nineties and anything was worth a shot.

So it is with serious (well, semi-serious) apologies to the Great State of Wisconsin that we include this recipe. It specifically calls for Canadian cheddar.

The Canadian provinces of Ontario and Quebec are noted for their fine cheddar cheeses. Smoother and creamier than cheddar produced in other countries, Canadian cheddar cheese has been exported to the United States since the nineteenth century. This recipe, from a Vietnam War–era cookbook, can be garnished with sourdough croutons or bits of Canadian bacon to get a truly "north of the border" dish.

U.S. Marine Corps
uniform, Vietnam

FOR AN ARMY OF 100

RATIONS:
- 1 pound carrots, chopped
- 1 pound celery, chopped
- 1 pound onions, dry, chopped
- 1 pound butter or chicken fat
- $3/4$ cup cornstarch
- $3/4$ quart flour, wheat, hard
- 1 tablespoon paprika
- 2 teaspoons pepper
- 3 tablespoons salt
- 2 gallons chicken stock
- 2 gallons hot water
- 2 gallons milk, evaporated (undiluted)
- 2 pounds cheddar cheese, shredded
- $1/2$ cup parsley, chopped

FOR AN ARMY OF 10

RATIONS:
- $1/4$ cup carrots, chopped
- $1/4$ cup celery, chopped
- $1/4$ cup onions, chopped
- 3 tablespoons butter, margarine, or chicken fat
- $3 1/2$ tablespoons cornstarch
- $1/4$ cup flour
- $1/4$ teaspoon paprika
- Pepper to taste
- $3/4$ teaspoon salt
- 3 cups chicken stock
- 3 cups hot water
- 3 cups evaporated milk (undiluted)
- $3/4$ cup cheddar cheese, shredded
- $2 1/4$ teaspoons parsley, chopped

ORDERS: Peel, wash, and chop carrots, celery, and onions finely. Melt butter or chicken fat in stockpot. Add carrots, celery, and onions. Mix well. Cook 5 minutes and remove from heat. Blend in cornstarch, flour, and seasonings. Add chicken stock and water, stirring constantly. Return to heat and cook until mixture thickens. Just before serving, add milk and cheese, stirring constantly until cheese is melted and thoroughly blended. Wash and chop parsley finely, add to soup. Serve hot. DO NOT BOIL.

CELERY SALAD
WORLD WAR I

The ancient Greeks considered celery to be the food of the gods (hence the phrase "Holy Celery!"). The Romans thought it was hot stuff, too; but they used it primarily as a medicine. It did not enter menus as a food in its own right until late in the nineteenth century.

This recipe, from a World War I cookbook, takes celery from the realm of crudités, or companion to buffalo wings, to the star of a salad. This is an interesting combination of ingredients that will certainly be a topic for discussion at your table, particularly if any of those ancient Greeks should show up.

FOR AN ARMY OF 60

RATIONS: 12 pounds celery, diced finely
2 pounds mashed potatoes
2 pounds bacon grease or olive oil
1 pint vinegar
1 pint water
2 ounces mustard (dry)
12 hard-boiled eggs (if desired)
Cayenne pepper

FOR AN ARMY OF 6

RATIONS: 2 $\frac{1}{2}$ cups celery, diced finely
$\frac{1}{3}$ cup mashed potatoes
$\frac{1}{3}$ cup bacon grease or olive oil
3 tablespoons vinegar
3 tablespoons water
1 teaspoon mustard
1 hard-boiled egg
Cayenne pepper

ORDERS: Dice the celery finely, chop the eggs, and mix the two together. For the dressing, mash the potatoes thoroughly, add the bacon grease (or olive oil) with the vinegar very slowly, and add a little salt, with cayenne pepper and mustard. The sauce should then be of the consistency of cream or gravy.

We were stewed to death!

—Albert M. Ettinger,
in *A Doughboy with the Fighting 69th*
(In the early days of World War I, the troops were supplied with fresh beef, but they weren't supplied with terribly imaginative cooks. For days at a time, whole sides of beef would be chopped and thrown into stew and the stew, seemed endless.)

SLANG

Slush Fund
(Navy; War of 1812): "Slush" was slang for the leavings and grease left over when the cook was done. He would save all this and sell it to sailors who would put it to a variety of uses. The money the cook collected from the sale of his slush became his "slush fund" (this, too, was put to a variety of uses).

CLAM CHOWDER
VIETNAM WAR

Talk to any two people from the northeastern United States about "chowda" and a debate will likely break out. Boston, Manhattan, and Rhode Island all claim chowder as their own. Even California has a dog in the fight.

The Boston variety uses milk or cream, while the New York or Manhattan chowder uses tomatoes. The question of tomatoes or no tomatoes even reached the state legislature in Maine in 1939, when a bill was introduced to make it illegal to add tomatoes to the soup in the state. (And isn't it a good thing that Maine had solved all its other problems, including the Great Depression, so its legislature could debate such a thing? The bill was defeated, by the way.)

In 1851, Herman Melville wrote most adoringly of it in *Moby Dick*: "But when that smoking chowder came in, the mystery was delightfully explained. Oh, sweet friends! hearken to me. It was made of small juicy clams, scarcely bigger than hazel nuts, mixed with pounded ship biscuit, and salted pork cut up into little flakes; the whole enriched with butter, and plentifully seasoned with pepper and salt . . . we dispatched it with great expedition."

The military formalized its recipe before the start of World War I and neatly sidestepped the entire issue by including neither milk nor tomatoes in this recipe. The World War I instructions follow more closely the historical origins of the soup that was made with fresh water—here using beef stock. Boston clam chowder seems to have won out, though. It is part of the military cookbook today and even is included in the MREs served to our troops in the field.

FOR AN ARMY OF 100

RATIONS: 6 quarts clams
8 pounds potatoes
1 pound bacon, diced and browned
10 quarts beef stock
$1/2$ pound chopped onions, browned

FOR AN ARMY OF 10

RATIONS: 2 $1/2$ cups clams
1 $1/2$ cups potatoes
3 tablespoons bacon, diced and browned
3 $3/4$ cups beef stock
1 $1/2$ tablespoons chopped onions, browned

ORDERS: Cook the potatoes, bacon, and onions in beef stock until well done, add the clams and let come to a boil; thicken slightly with a flour batter and it will be ready to serve. Salt and pepper to taste and regulate the amount of beef stock so that when the soup is ready to serve there will be about 6 gallons (8 cups).

COLE SLAW
VIETNAM WAR

Cole slaw began its road to food stardom during the early days of the twentieth century. Improved packaging and transportation and the introduction of bottled mayonnaise gave it a boost. As did backyard picnics.

The name is derived from the Dutch *kool sla*, meaning "cabbage salad."

Today, cole slaw is made with a variety of ingredients, and the dressings can be either a creamy mayonnaise-based recipe or a vinaigrette type. Here are two recipes for cole slaw from the 1960s—a vinegar-based slaw and a creamy-dressing slaw.

FOR AN ARMY OF 100

RATIONS: 12 pounds cabbage, finely shredded

$1 \frac{1}{3}$ cups onions, finely minced

3 pounds sweet peppers, finely shredded

$2 \frac{1}{4}$ cups vinegar

2 cups salad oil

$\frac{1}{2}$ cup sugar

1 tablespoon salt

$\frac{1}{2}$ teaspoon pepper

1 cup tomato catsup

5 tablespoons celery seed (optional)

FOR AN ARMY OF 10

RATIONS: 8 cups cabbage, finely shredded

3 tablespoons onions, finely minced

$1 \frac{1}{4}$ cups sweet peppers, finely shredded

$3 \frac{1}{2}$ tablespoons vinegar

3 tablespoons salad oil

$2 \frac{1}{4}$ teaspoons sugar

$\frac{1}{4}$ teaspoon salt

Dash pepper

$1 \frac{1}{2}$ tablespoons tomato catsup

$1 \frac{1}{2}$ teaspoons celery seed (optional)

ORDERS: Toss cabbage, onions, and peppers together lightly. Combine vinegar and oil with seasonings. Stir briskly with a wire whip. Pour over vegetables; toss together lightly. Cover and refrigerate.

CREAMY COLE SLAW
VIETNAM WAR

FOR AN ARMY OF 100

RATIONS: $^3/_4$ cup nonfat dry milk
1 $^3/_4$ cups warm water
1 quart salad dressing
$^1/_2$ cup prepared
mustard
3 $^3/_4$ tablespoons salt
1 cup sugar
1 cup vinegar
16 pounds cabbage,
finely shredded

FOR AN ARMY OF 10

RATIONS: 3 $^1/_2$ teaspoons nonfat
dry milk
8 $^1/_4$ teaspoons warm
water
1/3 cup salad dressing
2 $^1/_4$ teaspoons
prepared mustard
1 teaspoon salt
1 $^1/_2$ tablespoons sugar
1 $^1/_2$ tablespoons
vinegar
10 cups cabbage,
finely shredded

ORDERS: Reconstitute milk. Add salad dressing and seasonings. Mix well. Add vinegar gradually; blend well. Pour over cabbage; toss lightly until well mixed. Cover and refrigerate.

RICE SOUP
PLAINS WARS

This is a traditional recipe that would have been prepared in garrison for a squad of troopers. This version calls for beef, but if you have some elk or antelope in your freezer, that would work, too.

RATIONS: 4 pounds fresh beef
2 pounds soup bones
1 gallon cold water
1 onion, sliced
$^3/_4$ pound rice
Pepper and salt to taste.

ORDERS: Put the meat and bones into a pot with water, 1 tablespoon of salt, and the sliced onion and cook for about 5 hours. Three-quarters of an hour before the soup is cooked, strain it through a colander, return it with the good meat to the pot. Stir the rice into the strained soup 30 minutes before it is cooked; stir frequently to prevent it from scorching or sticking to the bottom of the kettle.

CREAM OF ONION SOUP
KOREAN WAR

When most people think of onion soup, French onion soup au gratin comes to mind: a steaming crock, topped with a large crouton and melted cheese, and filled with a rich beef broth and onions.

That would be a little tough to pull off for 100 guys in a mess hall.

Still, onions are a staple in the military kitchen. They keep well, are flavorful, and are easy to use in large quantities. As cook, you can get the guys assigned to K.P. to chop the things; that way, you don't have to cry.

So the military used a variation on the basic creamed soup recipe by making onions the main ingredient. This version, from 1950, could be easily served in the mess hall, even with the military version of a crouton—sliced white bread and butter.

FOR AN ARMY OF 100

RATIONS: 7 pounds onions, thinly sliced
2 gallons boiling water
2 $^3/_4$ gallons beef stock
4 $^1/_2$ 14 $^1/_2$-ounce cans evaporated milk
10 tablespoons salt
Pepper to taste
1 pound fat, melted
1 pound sifted flour
1 pound carrots, chopped finely
1 cup parsley, chopped finely

FOR AN ARMY OF 10

RATIONS: 3 cups sliced onions
3 cups boiling water
4 $^1/_2$ cups beef stock
$^3/_4$ cup evaporated milk
1 tablespoon salt
Pepper to taste
3 tablespoons fat, melted
$^1/_3$ cup flour, sifted
$^1/_3$ cup carrots, chopped finely
1 $^1/_2$ tablespoons parsley, chopped finely

ORDERS: Add onions to enough boiling water to cover. Heat to boiling point; reduce heat and simmer about 30 minutes.* Combine beef stock, milk, remaining water, salt, and pepper. Add to onions, carrots, and finely chopped parsley. Mix melted fat and flour; stir until smooth. Add slowly to hot soup and mix thoroughly. Heat to boiling point; reduce heat and simmer 20 minutes or until soup is slightly thick, stirring constantly.
*Cooked onions may be run through a sieve (or food processor) before combining with other ingredients.

TOMATO AND RICE SOUP
WORLD WAR II

The tomato has had a varied history. Indigenous to South and Central America, this fruit was brought to Europe by the Conquistadors and found a home in the Mediterranean region.

Not everyone was as enthusiastic. In fact, in large areas of Europe and in America, most people believed tomatoes to be poisonous. It wasn't until the early part of the nineteenth century that tomatoes came to be a staple. By the time of the War of 1812, Creole cooks in the South and New Englanders in Maine had incorporated the tomato into their recipes.

This simple recipe comes from an Army manual published in 1935. This soup can be varied with spices, such as cayenne pepper or basil, or enhanced with the addition of meats or seafood, to make a complete meal.

FOR AN ARMY OF 100

RATIONS: 2 No. 3 cans or
6 pounds fresh
tomatoes
2 pounds rice
7 gallons beef stock
Salt and pepper
to taste

FOR AN ARMY OF 10

RATIONS: 1 $\frac{1}{4}$ cups canned
tomatoes
$\frac{1}{3}$ cup rice
1 $\frac{1}{2}$ cups beef stock
Salt and pepper
to taste

ORDERS: Chop the tomatoes thoroughly and mix all ingredients. Season to taste, adding a small piece of garlic. Boil for 1 or 2 hours. Add enough beef stock 10 minutes before serving to make 10 gallons (1 gallon).

DEVILED HAM SANDWICHES
VIETNAM WAR

Since there are no devils (or gremlins or anything nefarious, for that matter) in military kitchens, the Army felt it was best to import them.

Deviled ham has long been a clever way to use up any leftovers from a baked ham dinner. It is easy and always a crowd pleaser.

FOR AN ARMY OF 100

RATIONS: 1 $\frac{1}{2}$ cups nonfat
dry milk
4 $\frac{1}{2}$ cups warm water
7 $\frac{1}{2}$ quarts cooked
ham, ground
3 cups sweet pickle
relish
4 tablespoons ground
mustard
1 $\frac{1}{2}$ quarts salad
dressing
1 quart butter
or margarine
200 slices bread

FOR AN ARMY OF 10

RATIONS: 7 teaspoons nonfat
dry milk
$\frac{1}{2}$ cup warm water
3 cups cooked ham,
ground
$\frac{1}{3}$ cup sweet pickle
relish
1 $\frac{1}{2}$ teaspoons ground
mustard
$\frac{3}{4}$ cup salad dressing
$\frac{1}{3}$ cup butter
or margarine
20 slices bread

ORDERS: Reconstitute milk; set aside to cool. Combine ham and relish; mix together lightly. Combine milk, mustard, and salad dressing; add to ham mixture. Spread slices of buttered bread with 1/3 cup filling each, top with second slices of buttered bread.

Huey helicopter crew
chief helmet, front views

FISH CHOWDER
PLAINS WARS

This is a traditional recipe that would have been prepared by a squad of men sitting around their campfire.

The recipe calls for the use of "hard bread." During the Civil War, this came to be universally known (and pretty much universally hated) as hardtack. (There's a recipe for making hardtack in Chapter 6.)

RATIONS: $^1/_2$ pound salt pork
4 onions
6 potatoes
3 pounds fish
$^1/_2$ pound hard bread
(or unsalted crackers)
Salt and pepper

ORDERS: Cleanse and cut the pork into thin slices; also slice the onions. Put the pork and onions together into a pot and fry them brown; then season lightly with salt and plenty of pepper. Slice the potatoes and lay them in cold water until wanted. Wash the fish and cut it into small pieces; soak the hard bread in water until tender. When the pork and onions have browned and been seasoned, add a layer of fish; on the fish a layer of potatoes; on the potatoes a layer of crackers, repeating the process until the kettle is nearly full. Set over a gentle fire, let it heat gradually, and simmer until done.

NOTE: Cleansing the salt pork would entail scraping any moldy bits or blackened edges from the slab. The rind, if thick, could also be cut away.

I hope Your Excellency is doing all in Your power to supply your half Starved Fellow Citizens. Flour, Rum, and Droves of Bullocks, should without delay be forwarded to this Army, or the Southern Department will soon want one to defend it.
—Horatio Gates to Virginia Governor Thomas Jefferson, 1780

MULLIGATAWNY SOUP
VIETNAM WAR

"Mulag-Tawny" soup was popular with British seafarers of the East India Company during the seventeenth and eighteenth centuries. The public houses on shore added it to their fare, and from there it slipped into general usage.

A spicy soup, mulligatawny usually has chicken stock as its base but can be made as a vegetarian soup, using vegetable stock.

FOR AN ARMY OF 100

RATIONS: 1 pound onions
1 pound sweet peppers, chopped
1 pound butter
13 $\frac{1}{2}$ ounces flour, wheat, hard
5 $\frac{1}{2}$ gallons chicken stock
1 $\frac{1}{2}$ pounds apples, chopped
$\frac{1}{2}$ pound carrots, chopped
1 pound celery, chopped
3 quarts canned tomatoes (1 No. 10 can)
$\frac{1}{4}$ teaspoon cloves
1 $\frac{1}{2}$ tablespoons curry powder
2 teaspoons black pepper
1 $\frac{1}{2}$ tablespoons salt

FOR AN ARMY OF 10

RATIONS: $\frac{1}{4}$ cup onions
$\frac{1}{4}$ cup green or red peppers
3 tablespoons butter or margarine
$\frac{1}{4}$ cup all-purpose flour
9 cups chicken stock
$\frac{1}{2}$ cup apples, chopped
2 carrots, sliced
$\frac{1}{3}$ cup celery, diced
1 $\frac{1}{4}$ cups tomatoes
Dash cloves
$\frac{1}{8}$ teaspoon curry powder*
$\frac{1}{8}$ teaspoon black pepper
$\frac{1}{3}$ teaspoon salt

ORDERS: Peel, wash, and chop onions finely. Remove stem, seeds, and white membrane from peppers; wash and chop finely. Melt butter in stockpot. Add onions and peppers, fry until onions are light yellow. DO NOT BROWN. Add flour and stir until smooth. Add stock, stirring constantly, and bring to a boil. Wash, peel, and core apples, cut into 1/4-inch pieces. Scrape, wash, and cut carrots into 1/4-inch pieces. Remove leaves and root ends of celery; wash thoroughly and cut into 1/4-inch slices crosswise of stalk. Add apples, carrots, celery, tomatoes, and seasonings. Bring to a boil; reduce heat and simmer for 35 minutes or until vegetables are tender.

*The curry powder and pepper can be adjusted to taste and the amount of spice you desire.

SALMON BISQUE
KOREAN WAR

"Bisque" was originally one of those catch-all phrases meaning it has a little bit of everything thrown in. In its original form bisque was a thick soup made from bits of offal.

In the military, bisque was a seafood soup made from canned fish or lobster. Serve this satisfying soup on October 19, National Seafood Bisque Day.

FOR AN ARMY OF 100

RATIONS: 2 pounds celery, sliced
1 pound onions,
dry, chopped
2 cups parsley, chopped
1 $\frac{1}{2}$ pounds butter
2 pounds flour,
wheat, hard
2 tablespoons paprika
2 teaspoons black
pepper
6 tablespoons salt
3 gallons hot water
3 quarts canned
tomatoes
(1 No. 10 can)
10 pounds canned
salmon
(10 No. 1 tall cans)
1 $\frac{1}{4}$ gallons milk,
evaporated
(undiluted)

FOR AN ARMY OF 10

RATIONS: $\frac{3}{4}$ cup celery, sliced
$\frac{1}{4}$ cup onions, chopped
3 tablespoons parsley,
chopped
$\frac{1}{4}$ cup butter
$\frac{3}{4}$ cup all-purpose flour
$\frac{1}{4}$ teaspoon paprika
Pepper to taste
1 $\frac{1}{2}$ teaspoons salt
4 $\frac{3}{4}$ cups hot water
1 $\frac{1}{4}$ cups tomatoes
1 $\frac{1}{2}$ cups salmon
(16 ounces)
1 $\frac{2}{3}$ cups evaporated
milk (undiluted)

ORDERS: Remove leaves and root ends of celery. Separate stalks and wash thoroughly. Cut into 1/8-inch slices crosswise of stalk. Peel, wash, and chop onions finely. Trim, wash, and chop parsley finely. Melt butter in stockpot. Add celery, onions, and parsley; cook 5 minutes, stirring occasionally. Add flour, paprika, pepper, and salt. Blend well. Add water, stirring until well blended. Add tomatoes and bring to a boil. Reduce heat and simmer 15 minutes, stirring occasionally. Remove bones and dark skin from salmon. Break salmon into small chunks (do not drain). Add salmon to the hot mixture. Cook 5 minutes. Just before serving, slowly add the milk to the mixture, stirring constantly. Heat to serving temperature. DO NOT BOIL.

NAVY BEAN SOUP
WORLD WAR II

The white or "Navy" bean has been traveling with the Navy pretty much ever since we've had a Navy. Sea voyages were long and arduous (hitting 10 knots of speed was a really big deal), and most fresh foods just wouldn't keep. Dried or preserved foods, like beans and smoked ham, would be daily fare toward the end of the journey when fresh rations had been consumed. Soup, especially, made these dried foodstuffs more palatable, and bean soup was born.

FOR AN ARMY OF 100

RATIONS: $3 \frac{1}{2}$ quarts dry
white beans
7 gallons ham stock
and ham bones
$2 \frac{3}{4}$ cups shredded
carrots
$4 \frac{1}{2}$ cups finely
chopped onions
2 teaspoons pepper
2 cups flour, sifted
$\frac{3}{4}$ quart cold water

FOR AN ARMY OF 10

RATIONS: $1 \frac{1}{2}$ cups dry
white beans
$10 \frac{1}{2}$ cups ham stock
and ham bones
$\frac{1}{2}$ cup shredded
carrots
1 cup finely chopped
onions
Dash pepper
3 tablespoons flour,
sifted
$\frac{1}{2}$ cup cold water

ORDERS: Pick over and wash beans. If using old beans, soak 3 to 4 hours before cooking. Add ham stock and bones. Heat to boiling point; cover and simmer 2–3 hours or until beans are tender. If necessary, add more hot water. Remove ham bones. Add carrots, onions, and pepper. Simmer for 30 minutes. Blend flour and water to make a paste. Stir into soup and cook 10 minutes longer.

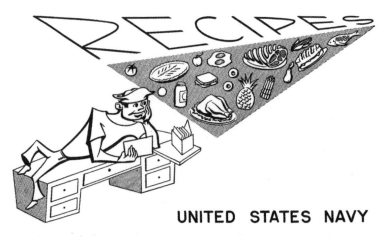

UNITED STATES NAVY

PEPINO SALAD
KOREAN WAR

The pepino melon was as popular in the Philippines during the World War II era as it is today. It is a teardrop-shaped fruit that is much like a cucumber and can be used in most recipes calling for cucumber.

Prior to the Japanese invasion of the Philippines, General Douglas MacArthur and his family lived in a suite at the Hotel Manila. Officially, this recipe found its way into the military manuals to take advantage of a plentiful food near the tropical outposts, but perhaps it was goaded along just a bit by the general's reported affinity for the taste.

FOR AN ARMY OF 100

RATIONS: 30 pounds pepino
36 hard-boiled eggs
3 pounds onions, sliced
$\frac{1}{2}$ cup salad oil
$\frac{1}{2}$ pint vinegar
2 tablespoons sugar
$\frac{1}{2}$ cup mustard
Salt and pepper to taste

FOR AN ARMY OF 10

RATIONS: 3 pounds pepino or cucumber
4 hard-boiled eggs
$1\frac{1}{4}$ cups onions, sliced
$2\frac{1}{4}$ tablespoons salad oil
$1\frac{1}{2}$ tablespoons vinegar
$\frac{1}{2}$ teaspoon sugar
$2\frac{1}{4}$ tablespoons mustard
Salt and pepper to taste

ORDERS: Wash, peel, and slice pepino or cucumber. Slice hard-boiled eggs and add eggs and onions to pepino or cucumber. Add vinegar, salad oil, sugar, mustard, salt, and pepper and mix; first mixing 10 minutes before serving time.

The general must be first in the toils and fatigues of the army. . . . He waits until the army's wells have been dug and only then drinks; until the army's food is cooked before he eats.

—Sun Tzu, *The Art of War*

PICCALILLI SALAD
WORLD WAR I

Piccalilli is a traditional Indian vegetable pickle. Also known as chow chow, and popular in Great Britain, it is customarily served as a savory accompaniment to meat.

This World War I–era recipe leaves the amount of seasoning up to the cook; that was fairly common in the military's cookbooks at the time. And we leave it that way here so you, too, can experiment a bit with those in your chow line.

FOR AN ARMY OF 60

RATIONS: 3 pounds cabbage, minced
3 quarts tomatoes, minced
3 pounds onions, minced
3 pounds pickles (issue), minced
$\frac{1}{2}$ quart vinegar
Seasonings: salt, cayenne pepper, cloves
Water

FOR AN ARMY OF 6

RATIONS: $\frac{2}{3}$ cup cabbage, minced
1 $\frac{1}{4}$ cups tomatoes, minced
$\frac{2}{3}$ cup onions, minced
$\frac{2}{3}$ cup pickles, minced
3 tablespoons vinegar
Salt, cayenne, pepper, and cloves to taste
Water

ORDERS: Mix all ingredients well; season with salt, cayenne pepper, and cloves, and add sufficient water to make 2 gallons (4 cups). Serve with baked beans or meat of any kind.

SELECTED MEN CLEANING THEIR MESS KITS, CAMP MEADE, MD.

You're in the Army now, boys—cleaning mess kits following their first meal after induction as the United States enters World War I.

POTATO SOUP
WORLD WAR II

The Army introduced automated potato peelers in 1959, thus ending years of hackneyed gags about K.P. and mounds of potatoes. Not to worry, though. There will always be pots to be scrubbed and floors to be mopped and dishes to be done.

You may wish to assign one of your soldiers to K.P. when you make this soup recipe from the World War II era.

FOR AN ARMY OF 100

RATIONS: 10 pounds diced
   potatoes
   7 gallons beef stock
   3 pounds onions,
   chopped and browned
   2 cans evaporated milk
   2 pounds fat, butter
   preferred
   1 pound flour,
   browned in fat
   Salt and pepper
   to taste

FOR AN ARMY OF 10

RATIONS: 1 pound diced
   potatoes
   10 cups beef stock
   $3/_4$ cup onions,
   chopped and
   browned
   $1/_2$ cup evaporated milk
   $1/_2$ cup fat, butter
   preferred
   $1/_4$ cup flour
   Salt and pepper
   to taste

ORDERS: Boil the potatoes in the stock until well done, then pass through a colander and bring to a boil again. Thicken with flour batter. Add the chopped onions and evaporated milk. Add enough beef stock 10 minutes before serving to make 10 gallons (1 gallon).

On a 1943 inspection tour in North Africa, General Dwight D. Eisenhower stops at the roadside for chow. His C-rations were heated on the engine block of his jeep.

SANDWICHES AND SANDWICH FILLINGS
WORLD WAR II

There are many different stories for the creation of the sandwich. The legend of England's Earl of Sandwich creating the first bread-and-meat finger food is familiar to many. But there are references to people filling the gap between two pieces of bread with meat and cheese long before Lord Sandwich in the eighteenth century.

Whatever the origins, the sandwich's popularity took off in the United States when the widespread availability of presliced bread made the sandwich a quick and easy meal. Slap some meat and cheese between the bread and presto! Instant meal!

The military decided to go one better. Someone must have been none too happy with overtime duty to come up with some interesting combinations for sandwich fillings. We have listed a few of these, taken directly from the War Department's 1942 TM-405, *Technical Manual for the Army Cook.*

BACON AND PEANUT BUTTER—
chopped bacon mixed with peanut butter

CHEESE AND PEANUT BUTTER—
chopped cheese, peanut butter, and mustard

DRIED BEEF AND CHEESE—
chopped cheese, evaporated milk, dried shredded beef, horseradish, and pepper

BEAN RAREBIT—
baked beans, chopped cheese, chopped onions, salt, pepper, and catsup

NUT AND RAISIN—
chopped nuts, chopped raisins, mayonnaise

TUNA FISH AND BEET—
flaked tuna, minced cooked beets, mayonnaise, salt, and pepper (can also substitute salmon or sardines)

CHEESE AND BACON—
chopped cheese, chopped cooked bacon, pimientos, mayonnaise, pickle relish, and lettuce

ST. PATRICK'S SOUP
SPANISH-AMERICAN WAR

The meat to be used in this recipe was unspecified (as was, frankly, quite a bit of the meat served to the troops during the Spanish-American War. See page 48). We propose that to get an Irish flavor, you use corned beef.

FOR A PLATOON OF 20

RATIONS: 6 pounds meat and fat
1 large cabbage
6 pounds potatoes
1 pound flour
1 pound onions
6 ounces salt
1 pound celery
1 pound turnips
6 tablespoons vinegar
1 pound carrots
3 $\frac{1}{2}$ gallons water

FOR A PLATOON OF 10

RATIONS: 3 pounds meat and fat
$\frac{1}{2}$ large cabbage
3 pounds potatoes
$\frac{1}{2}$ pound flour
$\frac{1}{2}$ pound onions
3 ounces salt
$\frac{1}{2}$ pound celery
$\frac{1}{2}$ pound turnips
3 tablespoons vinegar
$\frac{1}{2}$ pound carrots
1 $\frac{3}{4}$ gallons water

ORDERS: Cut the meat into pieces 1-inch square and the fat into smaller pieces; place in the boiler; when warm add vegetables (except the potatoes) cut very small; stir so that they do not burn; when they are on the point of doing so, add the water by degrees. Peel potatoes, put them in a net, and place in the boiler; when done take them out and mash them; after the soup has been boiling 2 hours, add the potatoes, with the seasoning and flour mixed, and the vinegar; boil slowly for 30 minutes, keep stirring, and serve.

American soldiers in the Spanish-American War

CRUNCHY VEGETABLE BURRITO
OPERATION IRAQI FREEDOM

Here's another example of the military's continuing efforts to provide healthy choices for contemporary tastes. Tex-Mex and yogurt don't usually go together, but the combination works well here.

This is a great low-calorie meal for a busy family on the run. Only 280 calories in this sandwich makes it a great choice for lunch or a light supper.

ORDERS: Combine yogurt, ranch dressing, garlic powder, chili powder, and cumin. Blend well. Refrigerate for later use. Combine kidney beans, sweet potatoes, tomatoes, broccoli, green onions, and jalapeno peppers. Toss vegetables in refrigerated dressing until well coated.

Wrap tortillas in foil; place in a warm oven about 150° or in a warmer for 15 minutes or until warm and pliable. Place about $^2/_3$ cup of the vegetable mixture on warm tortilla. Top with 2 tablespoons cheese. Spread evenly in center of tortilla. Fold up sides of tortilla; fold up front of tortilla to cover filling; roll tightly to back of tortilla like a burrito; wrap with parchment, wax paper, or foil.

First lady Barbara Bush, wearing camouflage, joins a chow line during Operation Desert Shield just prior to the start of the Gulf War in 1991.

FOR AN ARMY OF 100

RATIONS: 2 quarts plus
3 $\frac{1}{2}$ cups plain,
nonfat yogurt
2 quarts fat-free
ranch dressing
1 tablespoon garlic
powder
1 tablespoon dark
ground chili pepper
1 tablespoon ground
cumin
1 gallon plus
1 $\frac{7}{8}$ quarts dark red
canned kidney beans
3 quarts plus
3 $\frac{3}{8}$ cups fresh
peeled, shredded
sweet potatoes
2 quarts plus
3 $\frac{3}{8}$ cups fresh
chopped tomatoes
1 gallon plus
$\frac{1}{2}$ quarts fresh
broccoli flowerets
1 quart plus
$\frac{1}{2}$ cup sliced
green onions
1 quart plus
$\frac{1}{2}$ cup fresh sliced
green peppers
1 $\frac{1}{2}$ cup canned sliced
jalapeno peppers
100 10-inch wheat
tortillas
3 quarts plus 1 cup
reduced-fat
Monterey Jack
cheese, shredded

FOR AN ARMY OF 10

RATIONS: 3 $\frac{1}{4}$ cups plain,
nonfat yogurt
2 $\frac{3}{4}$ cups fat-free
ranch dressing
$\frac{1}{2}$ teaspoon garlic
powder
$\frac{1}{2}$ teaspoon dark
ground chili powder
$\frac{1}{2}$ teaspoon ground
cumin
2 cups dark red
canned kidney
beans
1 $\frac{1}{2}$ cups peeled,
shredded sweet
potatoes
1 cup fresh chopped
tomatoes
1 $\frac{3}{4}$ cups fresh
broccoli flowerets
$\frac{1}{2}$ cup sliced green
onions
$\frac{1}{2}$ cup fresh sliced
green peppers
2 tablespoons sliced
jalapeno peppers
10 10-inch wheat
tortillas
1 $\frac{1}{4}$ cups reduced-fat
Monterey Jack
cheese, shredded

VEGETABLE SALAD
VIETNAM WAR

For a while after World War II, it seemed like Murphy was in charge. When troops sailed across the Pacific, the transport ships were loaded with fresh foods (a good thing). The men were able to chow down, since fresh milk and eggs, vegetables, and meats were on the daily menus.

Invariably, the fresh foods ran out about a week before the voyage did. Tough passages and heavy weather got involved on Murphy's side to ensure his first law ("What can go wrong, will go wrong") was fully enforced. And the military cook was forced to rely on canned and dehydrated foods for the balance of the trip.

This salad could easily be put together with canned goods on the shelf.

FOR AN ARMY OF 100

RATIONS: 3 quarts canned green beans

3 quarts canned sliced carrots

3 quarts canned peas

4 $^3/_4$ quarts sliced fresh celery

1 $^1/_2$ quarts onions, finely chopped

3 tablespoons salt

1 quart prepared French dressing

3 cups salad dressing

FOR AN ARMY OF 10

RATIONS: 1 $^1/_4$ cups canned green beans

1 $^1/_4$ cups canned sliced carrots

1 $^1/_4$ cups canned peas

1 $^3/_4$ cups chopped celery

$^2/_3$ cup onion, finely chopped

$^3/_4$ teaspoon salt

$^1/_3$ cup prepared French dressing

$^1/_4$ cup salad dressing

ORDERS: Drain beans, carrots, and peas well. Combine vegetables with celery, onions, salt, and French dressing; toss lightly. Cover and refrigerate 1 hour. Just before serving, mix in salad dressing.

Vietnam War–era
green beret

WALDORF SALAD
OPERATION IRAQI FREEDOM

Waldorf salad, a staple of brunch and luncheon tables for decades, was created in 1896 by Oscar Tschirky, the maitre d'hotel of the Waldorf Astoria in New York City. According to Cole Porter, it was the tops.

The original salad consisted of only apples, celery, and mayonnaise, but today raisins and walnuts have become regular items in the recipe.

FOR AN ARMY OF 100

RATIONS: 3 tablespoons nonfat
dry milk
$^3/_4$ cup plus 2 table-
spoons warm water
$^1/_2$ cup lemon juice
$^1/_4$ cup plus $^1/_3$ tablespoon sugar
1 quart plus
1 cup salad dressing
3 pounds celery,
chopped
1 pound walnuts,
shelled and chopped
9 pounds apples,
cored and diced
4 pounds lettuce

FOR AN ARMY OF 10

RATIONS: $^3/_4$ tablespoon
nonfat dry milk
1 $^1/_3$ tablespoons
warm water
2 $^1/_4$ teaspoons lemon
juice
1 $^1/_2$ teaspoons sugar
$^1/_2$ cup mayonnaise
or salad dressing
$^1/_2$ cup chopped celery
$^1/_2$ cup chopped
walnuts
3 $^1/_2$ cups chopped
apples
Lettuce for serving

ORDERS: Reconstitute milk. Combine lemon juice, sugar, and salad dressing. Add to milk. Mix well. Add celery, nuts, and apples to salad dressing mixture. Toss well to coat pieces. Place one lettuce leaf on each serving dish; add salad. Cover and refrigerate until serving.

Adding a little color to his galley, this Navy chef prepares a salad somewhere in the Persian Gulf, 1998.

Creamed Chipped Beef

Baked Tuna Fish and Noodles

Baked Chicken and Noodles

Baked Ham and
Spaghetti Pie

Baked Luncheon Meat with
Mustard Sauce

Baked Sausage Cakes
with Apples

Fish Birds

Baked Tandoori Chicken

Baked Chicken with
Mushroom Gravy

Beef Croquettes

Beef Jerky

Beef Porcupines

Caribbean Catfish

Chili con Carne

Chicken Tetrazzini

Cheddar Chicken and
Broccoli

Chop Suey Hash

Chuck Wagon Stew

Smothered Ham

Wooden Shad

Corned Beef Hash

Corn Meal Mush

Creamed Eggs

Deviled Clams

English Muffin French Toast

Greek Lemon Turkey Pasta

Ham and Lima Bean Scallop

Lobster Newburg

Milk Toast

Oatmeal Mush

Pineapple Chicken

Oriental Tuna Patties

Salmon Cakes

Salt Pork and Hard Bread

Scotch Woodcock

Shrimp Creole with Rice

Slow Roasted Rabbit

Slumgullion

Stew El Rancho

Sweet and Sour Frankfurters

CHAPTER 3
ENTREES

CREAMED CHIPPED BEEF
WORLD WAR II

This may be the most famous—and most maligned—dish the military has ever served up for its troops. It really does head the category, "What were they thinking?"

At its best it could be a creamy, delicious meal. And you can still find veterans who will tell you that this was their mess hall favorite (these are the same gung-ho types who tell you how much they enjoyed boot camp). At its worst, it was like putting wallpaper paste on a slice of bread. Even so, it is still sold in nice, convenient packages in the supermarkets.

It became known as SOS (let's call it "Stuff on a Shingle"), and most veterans have a story or two to back up that name.

The current military version has been updated for the twenty-first-century palate, and it calls for lean ground beef rather than the salty, dried beef that made this dish famous. But that wouldn't be any fun. Here's the original, as it appeared in the 1945 *Manual for Navy Cooks.*

FOR AN ARMY OF 100
RATIONS: 7 pounds dried sliced
    beef
5 gallons milk
1 quart fat, melted
2 $\frac{1}{2}$ quarts flour
1 $\frac{3}{4}$ tablespoons
    pepper

FOR AN ARMY OF 10
RATIONS: 3 cups dried sliced
    beef
7 $\frac{1}{2}$ cups milk
$\frac{1}{3}$ cup fat, melted
1 cup flour
$\frac{1}{2}$ teaspoon pepper

ORDERS: Cut beef into small pieces. Heat milk to boiling temperature. Blend fat and flour to smooth paste. Stir into milk. Cook, stirring constantly, until thickened. Add pepper. Stir in beef. Let simmer about 10 minutes. Serve over toast.

NOTE: Soak meat in water 15 to 20 minutes if too salty.

At most bases it was typical Army chow. Half the time we expected it to crawl off our plates.
—Bob Hope, in *Don't Shoot, It's Only Me*

SLANG

Willie
Canned corn beef; it was universally loved to be hated by the doughboys of World War I.

WILLIE
0 compound of
    wrecked flesh, rent
    and torn asunder,
How do we e'er
    digest thy potency,
    I wonder—
Cold, killed cattle
    pounded into paste,
Pressed into tins and
    shipped to us
    in haste.

Greedily we eat thee,
    hot or cold
    or clammish,
How welcomely thou
    thuddest in the
    mess tins of
    the famished.
0 leavings of a
    jackal's feast,
    0 carrion sublime,
No matter how we
    scoff at thee, we
    eat thee every time.

Ah, CORNED WILLIE.

—Sgt. H. W. White in
Stars and Stripes, 1919

BAKED TUNA FISH AND NOODLES
KOREAN WAR

Tuna Noodle Surprise has always been a bit of a scary thing.

The "surprise" was often that, no matter what it looked like, the casserole usually tasted pretty good. Nearly as often, however, there actually was a surprise of some sort hidden deep inside the thing, and you wouldn't learn of it until you were actually chewing on it. And any soldier who's been mustered in will tell you that not all surprises are good, particularly when they are sprung in the mess hall.

This recipe belongs to the first category.

FOR AN ARMY OF 100

RATIONS: 10 pounds noodles
6 tablespoons salt
3 gallons boiling
water
2 quarts diced celery
4 tablespoons
chopped onions
2 4-ounce cans
chopped pimiento
2 quarts cornflakes
4 tablespoons salt
Pepper to taste
18 12-ounce cans
tuna fish, flaked
1 pint fat, melted
1 pint sifted flour
6 14 $\frac{1}{2}$-ounce cans
evaporated milk
3 quarts water
(for milk)

FOR AN ARMY OF 10

RATIONS: 2 cups noodles
1 $\frac{3}{4}$ teaspoons salt
4 $\frac{1}{2}$ cups boiling
water
$\frac{1}{3}$ cup diced celery
1 tablespoon chopped
onions
1 $\frac{1}{2}$ tablespoons
pimiento
$\frac{3}{4}$ cup cornflakes
1 $\frac{1}{2}$ teaspoons salt
Pepper to taste
3 cups tuna fish,
flaked
3 tablespoons fat,
melted
1 $\frac{1}{2}$ tablespoons
sifted flour
1 cup evaporated milk
1 $\frac{1}{4}$ cups water

ORDERS: Add noodles to boiling water; boil 10 minutes. Drain well. Combine noodles, celery, onions, pimiento, cornflakes, salt, pepper, tuna fish, and fish liquid and oil. Mix melted fat and flour; stir until smooth. Mix milk and water; add to flour mixture. Heat to boiling point; boil 5 minutes or until thick, stirring constantly. Pour over fish and noodle mixture; mix well. Pour into well-greased baking pans. Bake in moderate oven (375º) for 40 minutes.

BAKED CHICKEN AND NOODLES
KOREAN WAR

Here we have a conundrum. This recipe calls for "New York dressed chicken." When shopping for the ingredients for this recipe, you may have some difficulty finding that at your local supermarket.

A New York dressed chicken is one that has most all of the feathers removed (rough-plucked), but the head, feet, and entrails have been left intact. Exactly why a naked chicken would be deemed ready for a night on the town in Manhattan isn't quite clear. The term seems to have been in wide usage around the turn of the twentieth century. Presumably, the definition of suitable attire was a little looser then.

A butcher will have it. And they may even have it at some places in Manhattan. New York dressed fowl was generally less expensive than a "fully dressed" bird.

Thanksgiving dinner 1950, near Kaechon, Korea. The field was cold and muddy the day after Thanksgiving when these men were finally able to break from action. But the food was hot, and the company was almost like family.

FOR AN ARMY OF 100

RATIONS: 245 pounds chicken
New York dressed
Salt (for chicken)
Water, boiling,
for chicken
8 pounds noodles
4 tablespoons salt
(for noodles)
5 gallons boiling
water (for noodles)
1 $\frac{1}{2}$ gallons
white sauce
1 pound chopped
onions
2 tablespoons salt
Pepper
Flour
2 pounds melted
butter
2 quarts bread crumbs
1 pound diced cheese

FOR AN ARMY OF 10

RATIONS: 4 pounds chicken,
whole fryers cut up
Salt
Water
$\frac{2}{3}$ cup noodles
1 teaspoon salt
Water
2 $\frac{1}{4}$ cups white sauce
$\frac{1}{4}$ cup onion
$\frac{1}{2}$ teaspoon salt
Pepper
Flour
$\frac{1}{3}$ cup melted butter
$\frac{3}{4}$ cup bread crumbs
$\frac{1}{3}$ cup shredded
cheese

ORDERS: Clean chickens. Add to boiling salted water. Heat
to boiling point; reduce heat and simmer until tender. Cool. Skim fat from broth. Remove meat from
bones; leave meat in large pieces. Add noodles
to boiling salted water; boil 10 to 15 minutes or
until tender. Drain well. Prepare white sauce; add
onions, salt, and pepper.

Mix flour and melted fat; stir until smooth. Add
1 1/2 gallons of reserved chicken broth (2 1/4
cups). Heat to boiling point; boil two minutes
or until thick, stirring constantly. Add noodles.
Combine white sauce and cooked chicken. Spread
a layer of noodles on the bottom of greased baking pan(s); add a layer of creamed chicken. Pour
melted butter over bread crumbs; mix crumbs and
diced cheese. Sprinkle over chicken.

Bake in a hot oven (400°) until mixture is heated
through and crumbs are light brown.

PASS THE EMBALMED BEEF, PLEASE

A sunny afternoon on the hills just outside Santiago, Cuba, in late June 1898. There's no breeze. The air is hot, the humidity stifling. You're about to go into battle, and you're scared. You're a trooper in a winter uniform (because that's all the Army has given you). You've just slogged through miles of muddy jungle. You're tired. Your wool shirt is itching. Nearly a quarter of your regiment is down with some kind of fever, and you're being eaten alive by mosquitoes. You're just miserable.

All that is the good news.

The bad news is that it's time to eat.

Your rations today, as they've been nearly every day since you left Tampa weeks ago, are tinned beef. The cans are painted red. You've been lugging them with you since you got off the ship, but you probably wouldn't have if you had known what was in them.

The beef had originally been packaged five years earlier for shipment to Asia as part of a contract to supply combatants in the Sino-Japanese War. These were the leftovers. When this Spanish-American War broke out, their original labels had been hastily covered with red barn paint. With the paint barely dry, they were shipped off to feed American troops.

This was long before the federal government began to inspect food-processing facilities. The horrors that Upton Sinclair would detail in *The Jungle* had yet to be exposed. Anything rated "Grade A" made it there by sheer accident.

To be fair, the contents were never intended to be eaten straight out of the can. They were to have been combined with potatoes, onions, and other vegetables with a broth and served in a stew. This would have disguised the preservatives added to the gristle, fat, and some even less-enticing parts of a cow that had been neatly tinned.

There were several problems with the whole stew idea. First, with the painted-over labels it was impossible to read the directions. Next, out in the field where troops were about to go into battle, there wasn't time to sit down and put together a stew. And, finally, the Army didn't bother to ship either stoves or cooking gear to Cuba.

There was yet another big problem. When this stuff was packed, it wasn't intended to spend prolonged periods in the sweltering holds of ships, or in soldiers' backpacks, or in the heat of a tropical Cuban jungle in the summer. Cans became so hot that, essentially, the contents began to cook. It was slow cooking—months long. When the tins were finally opened, usually in the field with nothing else available to eat, the contents stank to high heaven. They had turned to a greenish-brown, gooey mess.

Soldiers became sick even before they started to eat it. If they did eat it, and were able to keep it down, they became even sicker.

The complaints were long and loud and were reported by the newspapers covering the war. Allegations of diseased meat were made against Armour & Company and Libby's—charges and denials and countercharges, many with screaming headlines and exclamation points.

When the fighting was done, and it came time to bring the boys home, it was apparent that something wasn't quite right in the casualty figures. American war dead totaled 3,289. Of these, only 332 had been killed in battle; the rest (2,957) had died from disease. The newspapers claimed the tinned beef was, in large measure, to blame.

President McKinley didn't want to make a big deal out of it at the time because, well, we won. And that should have been it. But the newspapers of the day weren't about to let it go, and Congress was up in arms. So, McKinley had little choice but to appoint a special commission tasked with getting to the bottom of the allegations.

For nearly six months, the commission heard testimony from military and civilian experts (the commission actually lasted longer than did the war). Hearings produced little hard evidence of corruption or fraud. Then, almost at the last hour, Major General Nelson Miles stepped forward. Miles had

This advertisement for canned meats produced by the Libby, McNeill & Libby company appeared in *Harper's Weekly* and other popular magazines of the day during the Spanish-American War. Libby was one of the companies implicated in the "embalmed beef" scandal following the war.

A scene from the Armour & Company meat packing facility in 1893. This may have been the very beef that was canned and called "embalmed."

been the commanding general of the Army during the war and had personally led ground forces. He was a hero, and in a position to know what was going on. His word would be given credence.

His word was that there was something rotten in those cans. He reported instances of gristle, rope, and even dead maggots being found packed with the meat. But that wasn't the worst part.

The worst part came from a doctor on the general's staff who had reported that the refrigerated beef was just as bad as the tinned beef. Tests had shown, it was alleged, that the refrigerated beef contained boric acid and salicylic acid. Both acids, poisonous in any concentration, had been injected into the beef, it was alleged, as preservatives.

Or so the doctor said. The newspapers said it a little differently. "Preservatives" became "embalming fluid," and according to the newspapers, the Army had served "embalmed beef" to the troops.

Then the finger-pointing really began. Miles stuck to his testimony, but the doctor's notes couldn't be found, nor could his findings be replicated. Commissary General Charles Patrick Eagan, in charge of rations for the Army, took serious exception to the accusations. Very serious exception. In his testimony before the commission he not only denied the charges, he denounced Miles:

"I wish to force the lie back into his throat covered with the contents of a camp latrine."

There were reports that Eagan considered challenging Miles to a duel. Not really appropriate for the brotherhood of officers.

The newspapers loved it, of course. Reporters went from Miles to Eagan and back to Miles again. More charges and countercharges. Eagan was so outspoken in his statements that he was eventually censured. Since Miles was superior in rank, Eagan was charged with insubordination and court-martialed. The court found him guilty and recommended his dismissal from service.

McKinley commuted the sentence, merely suspending him from rank, with pay, for the remainder of his career. Eagan, who had joined the Army as a volunteer in 1862, retired in 1905 at full pay but without duty.

In the meantime, the commission decided to act. It took more testimony, but finally determined that it could not substantiate the charges of "embalmed beef" (which were never actually made beyond the front pages of the papers). Next, the commission censured Miles for bringing the whole thing up in the first place.

But the newspapers continued to howl. General Miles was, after all, a hero. His word should be given far more weight.

We can now imagine poor President McKinley rolling his eyes and heaving a mighty sigh, as he once again weighed in. This time he authorized the formation of a "Beef Court," composed entirely of career military officers, to investigate Miles's allegations.

The Beef Court swung into action, but this time around General Miles took a different tack. He all but disavowed his earlier testimony. He backpedaled. He couldn't remember. He qualified his statements. It finally got to the point that the Beef Court wasn't exactly sure what charges and allegations it was supposed to investigate. So it, too, censured Miles for starting all this fuss, and then it adjourned.

At this point in the narrative you, as reader, may have lost track of that guy on the hill outside Santiago with his oddly painted can of alleged beef. That's pretty much the point. Nearly everyone else lost track of him, and his tin, too.

BAKED HAM AND SPAGHETTI PIE
OPERATION IRAQI FREEDOM

Here's a combination you don't see every day: ham, spaghetti, and pie. Close your eyes for a moment and try to imagine it. Don't forget the bacon.

From the military cook's point of view, it does make sense, since ham and bacon are easily kept, and dried pasta has a long shelf life. This dish is fairly easy to produce in large quantities. The combination works.

FOR AN ARMY OF 100

RATIONS: 5 pounds precooked, chopped bacon
2 gallons prepared marinara sauce
2 gallons canned diced tomatoes, drained
$1/_2$ cup garlic powder
$1/_2$ cup Italian seasoning
2 quarts plus 1 $1/_8$ cups grated Parmesan cheese
10 pounds diced cooked ham
10 gallons boiling water
$1/_2$ cup salt
1 quart shredded mozzarella cheese

FOR AN ARMY OF 10

RATIONS: $1/_2$ pound precooked chopped bacon
3 cups prepared marinara sauce
3 cups canned diced tomatoes, drained
2 $1/_4$ teaspoons garlic powder
2 $1/_4$ teaspoons Italian seasoning
1 $1/_4$ cups grated Parmesan cheese
1 pound diced cooked ham
4 cups boiling water
2 $1/_4$ teaspoons salt
$1/_2$ cup grated mozzarella cheese

SAUCE: Combine bacon, marinara sauce, tomatoes, garlic, Parmesan cheese, and ham. Reserve for later use.

ORDERS: Add salt to boiling water. Quickly scatter spaghetti noodles into boiling water in small batches. This prevents the noodles from sticking together. Stir while adding noodles. Cook spaghetti 8 minutes. Stir frequently during cooking time. Drain immediately. Do not rinse. Combine hot pasta with sauce. Mix well. Put in pans. Cover with foil. Seal tightly. Bake in 350° oven for 45–50 minutes. Remove from oven and top with mozzarella cheese.

BAKED LUNCHEON MEAT WITH MUSTARD SAUCE
KOREAN WAR

Somehow, somewhen, the military seemed to fall in love with euphemisms. During the Gulf War, for example, troops were equipped with "leather personnel carriers" rather than boots, and Commanding General H. Norman Schwarzkopf spoke of "bovine scatology" during press briefings.

Here's another one. Nowhere, other than military cookbooks, is this stuff called "luncheon meat." According to the manufacturer, it is "Spiced Pork and Ham." According to official World War II–era documents, it stands for "Specially Processed Army Meat." Soldiers have still other theories.

In the supermarket, just look for the can that says SPAM.

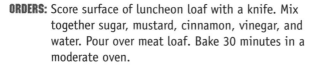

FOR AN ARMY OF 100

RATIONS: 15 6-pound cans luncheon meat
1 pint granulated sugar
4 tablespoons dry mustard
1 tablespoon cinnamon
1 pint vinegar
1 pint water

FOR AN ARMY OF 10

RATIONS: 3 pounds luncheon meat
3 tablespoons sugar
1 teaspoon dry mustard
$\frac{1}{4}$ teaspoon cinnamon
3 tablespoons vinegar
3 tablespoons water

ORDERS: Score surface of luncheon loaf with a knife. Mix together sugar, mustard, cinnamon, vinegar, and water. Pour over meat loaf. Bake 30 minutes in a moderate oven.

When in Korea, eat as the Koreans do. These GIs take a break with their interpreter for a large portion of rice (*bap* in Korean). Soldiers abroad usually chow down on the local diet.

BAKED SAUSAGE CAKES WITH APPLES
KOREAN WAR

This casserole can be served for breakfast, lunch, or dinner. The sweet fruit is a good foil for the spicy sausage. The military cook could easily prepare this simple dish in bulk for the long chow line.

FOR AN ARMY OF 100
RATIONS: 60 cooking apples
1 $\frac{1}{2}$ quarts brown sugar
30 pounds pork sausage

FOR AN ARMY OF 10
RATIONS: 6 cooking apples
$\frac{2}{3}$ cups brown sugar
3 pounds pork sausage

ORDERS: Pare and slice apples; place in baking pans. Sprinkle sugar over apples. Braise sausage cakes and drain off grease. Place sausage patties on top of sliced apples and bake in a moderate oven (350°) for 30 minutes or until done.

FISH BIRDS
KOREAN WAR

One can imagine an Air Force cook preparing this recipe and placing the toothpicks in precisely the right position to resemble the wings of a P-51 Mustang, generally considered the best fighter of World War II. These "Fish Birds" never bombed enemy positions in Europe, but they made a hit with the men on base. The bacon provides a nice flavoring for the fish as well as frying the outside a bit as it cooks.

FOR AN ARMY OF 100
RATIONS: 30 pounds fish fillets
4 tablespoons salt
1 tablespoon black pepper
1 pound bacon, sliced
12 pounds bread stuffing

FOR AN ARMY OF 10
RATIONS: 3 pounds fish fillet
1 $\frac{1}{2}$ teaspoons salt
$\frac{1}{4}$ teaspoon black pepper
$\frac{1}{4}$ cup bacon, sliced
4 $\frac{1}{2}$ cups bread stuffing

ORDERS: Remove skin and cut fillets into serving-size portions. Stuff with bread stuffing, roll and tie with string or fasten with toothpicks. Place in a well-greased baking pan. Sprinkle with salt and pepper. Place 1/3 strip of bacon on each roll. Bake at 375° for 30 minutes. Serve with a sauce.

BAKED TANDOORI CHICKEN
OPERATION IRAQI FREEDOM

The tandoor is a clay oven used in traditional East Indian cooking. Meat or poultry is marinated in yogurt and spices and then cooked in the tandoor over very high heat. Our recipe here adapts to the modern military kitchen but retains many of the components of the traditional Indian dish.

FOR AN ARMY OF 60

RATIONS: 3 quarts plain, low-fat yogurt
2 cups Dijon mustard
2 cups honey
$1/4$ cup plus $1/3$ tablespoon ground cumin
1 tablespoon salt
1 tablespoon garlic powder
1 tablespoon ground turmeric
1 tablespoon ground paprika
1 tablespoon hot sauce
31 $1/4$ pounds boneless, skinless chicken breasts
$1/4$ cup plus $1/3$ tablespoon nonstick cooking spray

FOR AN ARMY OF 6

RATIONS: 1 $1/4$ cups plain low-fat yogurt
$1/4$ cup Dijon mustard
$1/4$ cup honey
1 teaspoon ground cumin
$1/4$ teaspoon salt
$1/4$ teaspoon garlic powder
$1/4$ teaspoon ground turmeric
$1/4$ teaspoon ground paprika
$1/4$ teaspoon hot sauce
3 pounds boneless, skinless chicken breasts
Nonstick cooking spray

ORDERS: In a large mixing bowl, combine yogurt, mustard, honey, cumin, salt, garlic powder, turmeric, paprika, and hot sauce. Coat chicken breasts with yogurt mixture. Place chicken breasts on a lightly sprayed sheet pan. Lightly spray chicken breasts with cooking spray. Bake at 350° for 45–50 minutes or until chicken is fully cooked.

BAKED CHICKEN WITH MUSHROOM GRAVY
OPERATION IRAQI FREEDOM

Baked chicken was a staple of base kitchens during World War II. A relatively inexpensive main course, chicken could be baked in large quantities. Baked chicken was often served with mashed potatoes, but rice was also an accompaniment.

FOR AN ARMY OF 100

RATIONS: 82 pounds 8-piece cut chicken, skin removed
$\frac{1}{4}$ cup plus $\frac{2}{3}$ tablespoons nonstick cooking spray
3 tablespoons salt
2 tablespoons black pepper
1 quart plus 2 cups canned mushrooms
1 quart plus 3 $\frac{1}{2}$ cups warm water
1 $\frac{1}{2}$ cups nonfat dry milk
1 quart plus 2 cups flour
2 gallons plus 1 quart chicken broth
1 quart plus 2 cups chicken broth
1 tablespoon ground paprika

FOR AN ARMY OF 10

RATIONS: 8 pounds cut chicken, skin removed
Nonstick cooking spray
$\frac{3}{4}$ teaspoon salt
$\frac{1}{2}$ teaspoon pepper
1 cup canned mushrooms
1 cup warm water
$\frac{2}{3}$ cup nonfat dry milk
1 cup flour
3 $\frac{1}{2}$ cups chicken broth
1 cup chicken broth
$\frac{1}{4}$ teaspoon ground paprika

From Iraq to the Balkans, soldiers can't be choosy about their dining facilities; these Marines turn stacked boxes into tables at a field mess at Camp Monteith in Kosovo, in July 1999.

ORDERS: Wash chicken thoroughly under cold running water. Drain well. Remove excess fat. Place chicken, meat side up, on a lightly sprayed sheet pan. Sprinkle chicken with a mixture of salt and pepper. Lightly spray chicken with cooking spray. Bake at 350° for 25–30 minutes. Transfer chicken to roasting pan. Drain mushrooms and reserve liquid. Combine mushroom liquid and enough warm water to equal 7 1/2 cups (3/4 cup). Reconstitute milk with mushroom liquid and warm-water mixture. Lightly brown flour in a roasting pan on top of a gas range for 10–12 minutes. Use a wire whisk to stir and distribute flour for even browning. Cool; set aside for later use.

Heat chicken broth to a simmer in a stockpot; stir milk into hot broth. Blend flour and second chicken broth together to make a smooth slurry. Add slurry to broth and milk mixture. Bring to a boil. Cover; reduce heat; simmer 10 minutes or until thickened, stirring frequently to prevent sticking.

Stir chopped mushrooms gently into gravy; heat to a simmer. Pour gravy evenly over chicken in pans. Sprinkle paprika over each pan. Cover. Bake at 350° for 35–45 minutes or until done.

BEEF CROQUETTES
KOREAN WAR

"Cookie" is in his kitchen right after midday chow, surveying his domain. The assigned K.P.s have all been slowly and gloriously chewed out and are now meekly scrubbing pots and tables and floors so they will, upon inspection, reflect Cookie's bucolic countenance. All appears to be well.

So why is Cookie frowning?

Alas, there seems to be quite a bit of food left over. Meat, bread, mashed potatoes. Cookie doesn't like this. He doesn't like the idea that a cow, willing to die for his country, may have given his life in vain. He doesn't like his culinary creations spurned so. And we know that if Cookie isn't happy, ain't no one going to be happy.

So, what to do? Why, serve it all again, of course. Mix it up, disguise it with some batter, and hide it under the gravy. Then call it something fancy—say, "croquettes."

And all will be well in Cookie's realm.

Even tankers get to eat something other than K-rats. These crews stopped for a hot lunch on a mountain road near Tacaonhyon, Korea, in 1951.

FOR AN ARMY OF 100

RATIONS: 25 pounds beef,
cooked and ground
4 tablespoons salt
1 tablespoon pepper
5 quarts chopped
onion
2 $\frac{1}{2}$ pounds fat
(for frying)
2 quarts flour, sifted
2 quarts stock
30 eggs, slightly
beaten
5 quarts dry bread
crumbs
$\frac{1}{2}$ tablespoon
mace (optional)
1 14 $\frac{1}{2}$-ounce can
evaporated milk
1 pint water (for milk)
10 eggs, slightly
beaten
Flour, sifted (for rolling)
Bread crumbs
Fat (for frying)

FOR AN ARMY OF 10

RATIONS: 2 $\frac{1}{2}$ pounds beef,
cooked and ground
1 teaspoon salt
$\frac{1}{4}$ teaspoon pepper
2 $\frac{1}{2}$ cups chopped
onion
$\frac{2}{3}$ cup fat
(for frying)
$\frac{3}{4}$ cup flour, sifted
$\frac{3}{4}$ cup stock
3 eggs, slightly
beaten
2 cups dry bread
crumbs
Dash mace (optional)
3 $\frac{3}{4}$ teaspoons
evaporated milk
3 tablespoons water
(for milk)
1 egg
Flour, sifted (for rolling)
Bread crumbs
Fat (for frying)

ORDERS: Mix ground beef, salt, and pepper together. Fry onions until brown; add flour and mix well. Add stock gradually; heat to boiling point, stirring constantly. Cool; add slightly beaten egg, bread crumbs, mace, and ground beef; mix thoroughly. Refrigerate until thoroughly chilled. Mix milk and water; add beaten egg and mix well. Shape meat into croquettes; roll in flour and dip in egg and milk mixture. Roll in crumbs. Fry in deep fat (350°) 12 to 15 minutes or until golden brown. Serve hot.

BEEF JERKY
PLAINS WARS

During the Plains Wars of the latter half of the nineteenth century, troopers on the range often found themselves living off the land, in hostile territory, for extended periods. Often it wasn't healthy to build a cook fire, as the smoke, the aromas, and the light of the fire would draw the attention of predators and enemies alike from the still of the night.

Beef jerky, also known as pemmican, was a solution. Prepared in advance and carried in the cavalry's saddlebags, it would last long and could be eaten in the saddle or at night in a cold and dark camp.

This traditional recipe, most probably derived from Native American sources, does not specify the type of meat to be used. Beef, venison, buffalo, or perhaps even prairie dog, could be employed. Use your imagination to decide what species you would care to eat in such a circumstance.

The source of this particular version is *A Hand-Book for Mountain Scouting,* published in 1881 by Edward S. Farrow, assistant instructor of tactics at the United States Military Academy and former commander of Indian scouts in the Department of the Columbia.

Indian Wars
Service Medal

ORDERS: Take meat, without fat, and cut it into thin slices. Pound the meat and mix in melted fat and maybe dried fruit. Compress the mixture into cakes, strips or in bags. Dry the meat in the sun. It contains much nutriment in small compass, and is of great use in long voyages. A little salt added would make it more palatable to the civilized taste.

BEEF PORCUPINES
VIETNAM WAR

We don't want to get too graphic here, but the rice really is supposed to swell up and stick out of the meat. Really. When you're done, you're supposed to have little round pieces of meat with white things sticking out.

The usual method for cooking rice isn't all that complicated: Take some rice, throw it in really hot water, wait a bit, and then eat it. This is a little more sophisticated.

The idea here is to cook the rice inside the meatballs. As these meatballs cook, the rice puffs up and sticks out from the surface of the meat, making the meatballs look a like little porcupines. These can be served over egg noodles or rice (if at all).

FOR AN ARMY OF 100

RATIONS: 30 pounds ground beef
1 $1/2$ quarts chopped onions
6 tablespoons salt
1 $1/2$ quarts parboiled rice
1 quart sweet peppers, chopped
1 $1/2$ tablespoons garlic, chopped (optional)
4 quarts canned tomato paste
8 quarts water

FOR AN ARMY OF 10

RATIONS: 3 pounds ground beef
$2/3$ cup chopped onions
1 $3/4$ teaspoons salt
$2/3$ cups cooked rice
$1/3$ cup sweet peppers, chopped
$1/3$ teaspoon chopped garlic (optional)
1 $1/2$ cups canned tomato paste
3 cups water

ORDERS: Combine all ingredients, except tomato paste and water, thoroughly but do not overmix. Shape into 3 1/4 ounce balls, about 1 1/2 inches in diameter. Place 100 balls in each pan. Mix tomato paste and water. Pour an equal quantity over balls in each pan. Bake 1 1/2 hours or until done. Turn balls at least once during baking.

CARIBBEAN CATFISH
OPERATION IRAQI FREEDOM

Lots of herbs, lots of spices, and a generous combination of sharp flavors make this dish distinctive. You'll find it lighter and more interesting than some of the other baked fish recipes here.

FOR AN ARMY OF 100

RATIONS: 1 quart plus 2 $\frac{1}{8}$ cups chopped green peppers
$\frac{3}{4}$ cup margarine
1 quart plus 2 cups chopped onions
2 gallons plus $\frac{1}{2}$ quarts cubed white bread
2 tablespoons crushed oregano
1 tablespoon ground red pepper
3 tablespoons garlic powder
1 $\frac{1}{4}$ cups dry cilantro
1 $\frac{1}{2}$ cups lime juice
30 pounds catfish fillets
1 $\frac{1}{2}$ cups lime juice
$\frac{3}{4}$ cup melted margarine
3 tablespoons garlic powder
1 tablespoon ground red pepper
2 fresh limes

FOR AN ARMY OF 10

RATIONS: 1 cup chopped green peppers
3 $\frac{1}{2}$ teaspoons margarine
1 cup chopped onions
3 $\frac{1}{4}$ cups cubed white bread
$\frac{1}{2}$ teaspoon crushed oregano
$\frac{1}{4}$ teaspoon ground red pepper
$\frac{3}{4}$ teaspoon garlic powder
2 tablespoons dried cilantro
1 tablespoon lime juice
3 pounds catfish fillets
1 tablespoon lime juice
3 $\frac{1}{2}$ teaspoons melted margarine
$\frac{3}{4}$ teaspoon garlic powder
$\frac{1}{4}$ teaspoon ground red pepper
$\frac{1}{2}$ fresh lime

ORDERS: Sauté green peppers and onions in margarine or butter 10 minutes or until onions are transparent. Combine onion mixture with bread cubes, lime juice, cilantro, garlic powder, red pepper, and oregano; mix well. Place 1 1/4 ounces filling in the center of each catfish fillet, skin side up. Roll up and place seam side down in a staggered row in a large baking pan. Combine margarine or butter with lime juice. Add garlic powder and red pepper. Brush evenly over fish. If desired, sprinkle 1 tablespoon grated lime rind over fish. Bake at 350° for 35 to 40 minutes or until internal temperature reaches 165°.

CHILI CON CARNE
WORLD WAR I

They claim to know their chili in Texas. And in Cincinnati. They got herbs. And they got ingredients. They got special stuff that they throw in there. They got contests. And they create a whole lot of wind about how good it all is.

But this is the real stuff: just meat and peppers and beans. This is the way the doughboys in the trenches wanted it. And even today, there are those who will claim that it just doesn't get any better than this.

FOR AN ARMY OF 60

RATIONS: 15 pounds meat scraps
3 $\frac{1}{2}$ ounces chili
peppers, ground
3 $\frac{1}{2}$ quarts chili
(pink) beans

FOR AN ARMY OF 6

RATIONS: 1 $\frac{1}{2}$ pounds meat
scraps
2 $\frac{1}{4}$ teaspoons chili
powder
1 $\frac{1}{2}$ cups chili
(pink) beans

ORDERS: Trim all the fat from the meat and chop into half-inch cubes; place in a bake pan and fry in the same manner as beefsteak, but using a smaller amount of fat; cover with about 1 inch of beef stock; add the ground chili pepper and salt to taste. Run two-thirds of boiled chili beans through a meat chopper and mix all together.

Field Mess

This souvenir postcard shows a group of World War I doughboys sitting down for lunch in the field. The idea was to send it home: "Look, Ma, I'm eating right."

CHICKEN TETRAZZINI
VIETNAM WAR

It was San Antonio sportswriter Dan Cook who is credited with saying that it ain't over until the fat lady sings. Louisa Tetrazzini wasn't especially fat, but she certainly could belt out a tune. During the early decades of the last century, this Italian soprano was the toast of the opera world. Legend has it that this recipe was created in her honor during one loud and operatic visit to San Francisco.

FOR AN ARMY OF 100

RATIONS: 5 pounds spaghetti
3 gallons boiling water
6 tablespoons salt
1 cup chopped onions
1 cup chopped sweet
   peppers
1 $^1/_2$ quarts canned
   mushrooms
1 quart butter or
   margarine, melted
1 quart flour
1 $^3/_4$ cups chicken
   soup and gravy base
1 $^3/_4$ gallons water
2 $^7/_8$ cups nonfat
   dry milk
3 $^3/_4$ quarts warm water
2 $^3/_4$ cups chopped
   pimientos
1 teaspoon black pepper
2 gallons (10 29-ounce
   cans) cooked chicken
1 quart shredded
   cheddar cheese

FOR AN ARMY OF 10

RATIONS: $^1/_2$ pound spaghetti
4 $^1/_2$ cups boiling water
1 $^3/_4$ teaspoons salt
1 tablespoon chopped
   onion
1 tablespoon chopped
   sweet peppers
$^2/_3$ cup canned
   mushrooms
$^1/_3$ cup butter or
   margarine, melted
$^1/_3$ cup flour
3 tablespoons chicken
   soup or gravy base
2 $^1/_4$ cups water
$^3/_4$ cup nonfat dry milk
$^3/_4$ cup warm water
$^1/_2$ cup chopped
   pimiento
Dash black pepper
3 cups canned or
   cooked chicken
$^1/_3$ cup shredded
   cheddar cheese

ORDERS: Stir spaghetti into boiling salted water. Stir frequently. Cook about 15 minutes. Drain and set aside. Sauté onions, pepper, and mushrooms in butter or margarine 10 minutes or until tender. Combine flour and soup base; stir until well blended. Add to sautéed vegetables. Reconstitute milk; add gradually to flour and soup base mixture, stirring constantly. Simmer 10 minutes. Add pimientos, pepper, chicken, and spaghetti. Pour into casserole pan. Sprinkle cheese over mixture in pan. Bake at 450° for 20 minutes or until cheese is browned.

CHEDDAR CHICKEN AND BROCCOLI
OPERATION IRAQI FREEDOM

One of the really neat things about being in New York City during the 1950s was the wealth of restaurants and tastes to be found there. (Come to think of it, fifty years later that is still one of the neat things about being in New York City.) A restaurant that made its mark during the Eisenhower administration was a spot called Divan Parisien. Among the innovations to be found there was a dish called Chicken Divan. This recipe is a variation on the original. The Army's version produces a quick casserole with cheddar cheese, and includes rice. Not quite as neat as New York City, but not too far off, either.

FOR AN ARMY OF 100

RATIONS: 3 quarts plus $^3/_4$ cups chopped onion
1 gallon plus 1 $^1/_4$ quarts chopped celery
$^1/_4$ cup plus $^1/_3$ tablespoon nonstick cooking spray
2 gallons plus 2 quarts chicken broth
1 gallon water
3 quarts long-grain and wild rice
3 tablespoons salt
3 tablespoons garlic powder
2 tablespoons black pepper
18 pounds cooked diced chicken
2 gallons frozen chopped broccoli
2 quarts shredded cheddar cheese

FOR AN ARMY OF 10

RATIONS: 1 $^1/_2$ cups chopped onion
2 cups chopped celery
Nonstick cooking spray
3 $^2/_3$ cups chicken broth
1 $^1/_2$ cups water
1 $^1/_4$ cups long-grain and wild rice
$^3/_4$ teaspoon salt
$^3/_4$ teaspoon garlic powder
$^1/_2$ teaspoon pepper
2 cups cooked diced chicken
3 cups frozen broccoli
$^3/_4$ cup shredded cheddar cheese

ORDERS: Stir-cook onions and celery in lightly sprayed stockpot for 8 to 10 minutes or until tender, stirring constantly. Add broth, water, rice, salt, garlic powder, and pepper to cooked onions and celery. Bring to a boil. Cover tightly; reduce heat; simmer 20 minutes. There will be excess cooking liquid in cooked rice mixture. Stir chicken and broccoli into cooked rice mixture. Cover; simmer an additional 15 minutes. Pour mixture into baking pans. Cover with cheddar cheese. Bake at 400° for 3 minutes or until cheese is melted.

CHOP SUEY HASH
WORLD WAR I

There isn't too much that is authentically Chinese about this variation of the recipe. But that's probably as it should be, because there isn't much that is authentically Chinese about chop suey in the first place.

The whole thing got started in the 1890s, when Chinese diplomat Li Hongzhang visited New York City. As much as he wanted to be diplomatic, he just couldn't stand the food, and he would dine only in restaurants to be found in Chinatown. Newspapers of the day reported the great man's every move and, naturally, wanted to know what he had eaten in these authentic restaurants. "Chop suey" was the reply, and a craze swept the country (some estimates place the number of chop suey houses in New York alone at more than 400).

One suspects that the newspapers' collective leg was being pulled. Well, jerked, actually. Because there was no single thing known as chop suey. Literally, it means "bits and pieces" in Cantonese. In fact, the term itself didn't even show up in Chinese dictionaries until the 1990s. So chop suey is actually an authentic American-Chinese-New York way of making a buck by cobbling together leftovers. But it was a craze, one that the *Manual for Army Cooks*, published in 1916, seized upon. In the home kitchen, this casserole can be made in a large skillet or electric fry pan. By rendering the bacon in the oven, the cook would have enough shortening in the dish to cook and flavor the rest of the ingredients.

SLANG

Custard grenade
A guest ordering his dinner at a fashionable hotel just after the war:
"Noodle soup, veal cutlet with tomato sauce and a cream puff, please."
Now, the waiter had spent his time in the trenches at the front, so he told the chief, "Bowl of submarines, camouflage the calf and a custard grenade."

—Sergeant Major Edward D. Rose in *Khaki Komedy* (1918)

FOR AN ARMY OF 60

RATIONS: 4 pounds fat bacon, chopped fine
1 gallon onions, chopped fine
10 pounds cooked beef, coarsely ground
10 pounds turnips, cooked and chopped
3 cans corn
1 ounce chili powder
1 gallon soup stock
2 cans tomatoes

FOR AN ARMY OF 6

RATIONS: $3/4$ cup bacon, chopped fine
1 1/2 cups onions, chopped fine
1 pound cooked ground beef
2 cups turnips, cooked and chopped
$2/3$ cup corn
2 teaspoons chili powder
1 $1/2$ cups stock
$1/3$ cup tomatoes

ORDERS: Place the bacon in a large bake pan and put in the oven until well rendered; add the onions and fry until half done; add the other ingredients and bake for 1 hour.

CHUCK WAGON STEW
OPERATION IRAQI FREEDOM

This is a quick and easy casserole that somehow gives you the idea of hardened cowboys sitting around a campfire on the open range on a warm summer's evening, with little dogies quietly mooing in the distance and someone blowing on a harmonica. A long day on the trail. A little grit on your teeth. Everyone needs a shave. And probably a bath.

Actually, this isn't anything at all like that. But the Army calls it Chuck Wagon Stew, and they probably know more about it than we do.

It is good served over biscuits or mashed potatoes. In any case, bread and butter are a necessary accompaniment, along with a green salad or vegetable.

FOR AN ARMY OF 100

RATIONS: 15 pounds ground
             beef, 90% lean
             6 pounds chopped
             onions
             3 pounds chopped
             green peppers
             3 1/2 cups catsup
             6 gallons canned
             baked beans
             with pork

FOR AN ARMY OF 10

RATIONS: 1 $\frac{1}{2}$ pounds ground
             beef, 90% lean
             1 $\frac{3}{4}$ cups chopped
             onions
             1 cup chopped green
             pepper
             $\frac{1}{3}$ cup catsup
             9 cups canned baked
             beans with pork

ORDERS: Cook beef in stockpot with onions and peppers
            until it loses its pink color, stirring to break apart.
            Drain or skim off excess fat. Add catsup and beans
            to beef, onion, and pepper mixture. Stir well.
            Simmer for 20 minutes.

CORN MEAL MUSH
WORLD WAR I

This breakfast recipe has been a staple of military tables through a good portion of our history. Without a lot of variation, it was prepared in Navy galleys during the Revolution, cooked on the battlefields of Antietam and Gettysburg during the Civil War, and saw action on the Great Plains and during the Spanish-American War. Corn meal mush is about as American as it gets.

This is the World War I version. It would have served 60 hungry men and been part of a menu including apple butter, boiled eggs, bacon, potatoes, bread and butter, and coffee. You may want to consider a little brown sugar sprinkled over the top and a glass of milk or juice.

FOR AN ARMY OF 60

RATIONS: 6 pounds corn meal
1 $\frac{1}{2}$ pounds sugar (if not on the table)
1 ounce salt
4 gallons water

FOR AN ARMY OF 6

RATIONS: 1 $\frac{1}{2}$ cups corn meal
$\frac{1}{2}$ cup sugar
1 teaspoon salt
8 cups water

ORDERS: Allow the water to come a boil, add the salt (and sugar if not on the table) and the corn meal, meanwhile whipping well to prevent lumping. Cook for about 20 minutes and then allow to stand about the same length of time where it will remain hot. Place in vegetable dishes and serve hot with fresh or evaporated milk over it.

This is the most popular sport in camp.

World War I–era postcard claims eating was "the most popular sport in camp." Probably wasn't too far from right.

CREAMED EGGS
VIETNAM WAR

This breakfast casserole is simply hard-boiled eggs with a thin white sauce. It can be made in quantity, an attractive quality for the military cook. A fruit salad (see our recipe for Spiced Fruit Cup), along with whole-wheat toast, rounds out a hearty breakfast or brunch.

FOR AN ARMY OF 100

RATIONS: 11 $3/4$ quarts nonfat dry milk

9 $1/3$ quarts warm water

3 $3/4$ cups butter or margarine, melted

1 $1/2$ quarts sifted flour

4 $1/2$ tablespoons salt

144 hard-cooked eggs, sliced

FOR AN ARMY OF 10

RATIONS: $3/4$ cup nonfat dry milk

2 $1/2$ cups warm water

$1/3$ cup butter or margarine, melted

$2/3$ cup sifted flour

1 teaspoon salt

14 hard-cooked eggs, sliced

ORDERS: Reconstitute milk; heat to just below boiling. DO NOT BOIL. Blend butter or margarine, flour, and salt together; stir until smooth. Add mixture to milk, stirring constantly. Heat 5 to 10 minutes until thickened. Stir as necessary. Add eggs to sauce. Mix lightly.

This chow hall was under canvas in Vietnam. The troops came, armed, for breakfast.

DEVILED CLAMS
VIETNAM WAR

Like deviled eggs, the addition of a little hot sauce spices up this dish. The spices and sweetness of the chili sauce enhance the nippy finish of the hot sauce. Devil this recipe to your taste by adjusting the amount of hot sauce.

FOR AN ARMY OF 100

RATIONS: 8 cloves garlic, chopped
2 cups chopped onions
3 quarts chopped celery
1 quart butter or margarine
1 cup flour
3 tablespoons salt
1 tablespoon black pepper
1 tablespoon ground thyme
2 gallons thawed, shucked clams
20 eggs
$1/_2$ teaspoon hot sauce
1 cup chili sauce
9 $3/_4$ cups cracker crumbs
2 cups fresh parsley, chopped
1 $1/_2$ quarts bread crumbs
2 cups melted butter or margarine

FOR AN ARMY OF 10

RATIONS: 1 small clove garlic, chopped
$1/_4$ cup chopped onions
1 $1/_4$ cups chopped celery
$1/_3$ cup butter or margarine
1 $1/_2$ tablespoons flour
$3/_4$ teaspoon salt
$1/_8$ teaspoon black pepper
$1/_8$ teaspoon ground thyme
3 cups thawed, shucked clams
2 eggs
Dash hot sauce
1 $1/_2$ tablespoons chili sauce
1 $2/_3$ cups cracker crumbs
3 tablespoons parsley
$3/_4$ cup bread crumbs
3 $1/_2$ tablespoons melted butter or margarine

ORDERS: Sauté garlic, onions, and celery in butter or margarine until light yellow. Blend in flour, salt, pepper, and thyme. Drain clams; chop and add to flour mixture. Cook until thick, stirring constantly. Combine eggs, hot sauce, and chili sauce. Add to clam mixture, stirring constantly. Remove from heat. Add cracker crumbs and parsley to clam mixture. Place mixture into well-greased pans. Sprinkle buttered crumb mixture over top of clam mixture. Bake in a 400° oven for 10 minutes or until brown. Cut into squares for serving.

ENGLISH MUFFIN FRENCH TOAST
OPERATION IRAQI FREEDOM

If you didn't know what this recipe was from its title, you'd never figure it out from its title, because just about the entire title is a misnomer.

First of all, "English muffins" aren't. They aren't English and they do rather stretch the definition of muffin. They are a derivative (nice way of putting it) of an English crumpet. But true crumpets have the nooks and crannies on one of the outsides (rather than on both of the insides), and they are not nearly as doughy as English muffins. Traditionally, they are grilled over an open fire, not in a toaster.

Which brings us to the toast part. These aren't toasted. They're fried.

Finally, there's the French part. The name actually comes from Albany, New York. It seems that a tavern keeper there, one Joseph French, was the first in America to dip stale bread into egg and milk and fry it up. And, while he may have been one of America's all-time-great tavern keepers, he wasn't much of a grammarian. He just didn't bother with apostrophes. So, instead of calling it "French's toast," he dubbed it "French toast" without the possessive.

Other than that, though, it's fine.

FOR AN ARMY OF 100

RATIONS: 2 quarts plus
3 cups water
2 3/8 cups nonfat
dry milk
1 1/2 cups sugar
3 quarts plus 2 cups
whole frozen eggs
100 split English
muffins
2 ounces nonstick
cooking spray

FOR AN ARMY OF 10

RATIONS: 1 1/2 cups water
6 tablespoons nonfat
dry milk
2 tablespoons sugar
8 eggs
10 split English
muffins
Nonstick cooking spray

ORDERS: Place water in mixer bowl. Combine milk and sugar; blend well. Add to water; whip on low speed until dissolved, about 1 minute. Add eggs to ingredients in mixer bowl; whip on medium speed until well blended, about 2 minutes. Cut muffins in half; dip split muffins in batter 30 seconds. DO NOT SOAK. Lightly spray griddle with nonstick spray. Place muffins on griddle, cut side down. Grill about 3 minutes; turn, grill on crust side about 1 1/2 minutes.

GREEK LEMON TURKEY PASTA
OPERATION IRAQI FREEDOM

Please don't be misled.

The flavor of Greece, according to modern military cookery, is captured with this cunning combination of soy sauce and pasta. Mousaka? Filo pastry? Ripe black olives? Never heard of 'em. If you're talking Greek cuisine, you're talking turkey and lemon. The intent of this hot casserole is Greek. Lemon and spinach, a delightful combination, go well with the turkey and pasta. The soy sauce marinade, along with more lemon and garlic, does enhance the turkey.

So it's Greek. Don't be misled. Please.

FOR AN ARMY OF 100

RATIONS: 1 cup soy sauce
1 cup lemon juice
$\frac{1}{4}$ cup plus 2 $\frac{1}{3}$ tablespoons fresh minced garlic
$\frac{1}{4}$ cup plus 2 $\frac{1}{3}$ tablespoons ground black pepper
$\frac{1}{4}$ cup plus 1 tablespoon grated lemon rind
16 pounds boneless turkey, white and dark meat
8 gallons water
$\frac{1}{4}$ cup plus $\frac{1}{3}$ tablespoon salt
3 gallons plus 1 quart dry rotini pasta
2 $\frac{1}{2}$ cups water
2 cups cornstarch
2 gallons plus 2 quarts chicken broth
1 tablespoon nonstick cooking spray
1 gallon plus 2 $\frac{1}{2}$ quarts frozen spinach
2 $\frac{1}{2}$ cups frozen spinach
2 quarts plus 2 $\frac{3}{8}$ cups sliced onions
$\frac{3}{4}$ cup sliced onions
2 $\frac{1}{2}$ cups lemon juice
$\frac{1}{4}$ cup lemon juice

FOR AN ARMY OF 10

RATIONS: 1 tablespoon soy sauce
1 tablespoon lemon juice
2 $\frac{1}{2}$ teaspoons fresh minced garlic
2 $\frac{3}{4}$ teaspoons ground black pepper
2 teaspoons lemon rind
1 $\frac{1}{2}$ pounds boneless turkey, white and dark meat
6 cups water
1 $\frac{1}{4}$ teaspoons salt
4 $\frac{1}{2}$ cups dry rotini pasta
$\frac{1}{2}$ cup water
$\frac{1}{4}$ cup cornstarch
4 $\frac{1}{2}$ cups chicken broth
Nonstick cooking spray

ORDERS: Combine soy sauce, lemon juice, garlic, pepper, and lemon rind. Mix well. Slice turkey into 1/2-inch slices; cut slices into 1/2-inch strips, 2 to 3 inches in length. Add marinade. Toss to coat turkey evenly. Cover and refrigerate. Bring water to a boil; add salt. Slowly add rotini while stirring until water boils again. Cook 10 to 12 minutes or until almost tender; stir occasionally. Drain. Rinse in cold water. Drain thoroughly. Dissolve cornstarch in water. Prepare chicken stock according to package directions. Spray stockpot or large skillet with nonstick cooking spray. Add turkey and marinade. Stir-cook until turkey is no longer pink. Add spinach and stock; bring to a boil. Reduce heat; slowly add cornstarch mixture, stirring constantly, about 5 minutes or until slightly thickened. Add green onions, lemon juice, and rotini, stirring until ingredients are well distributed.

A birthday treat for the Marine Corps in Iraq. This Iraqi soldier prepares lamb kabobs in the city of Fallujah during November 2005 as part of the Marines' birthday party.

HAM AND LIMA BEAN SCALLOP
OPERATION IRAQI FREEDOM

In the original military recipe for this dish, the molasses and onions are suggested as a variation. However, the sweetness of the molasses and the onion flavor really add something to the casserole.

FOR AN ARMY OF 100
RATIONS: 12 pounds dried lima beans
Water
20 pounds cooked, sliced ham
4 tablespoons salt
$\frac{1}{2}$ tablespoon pepper
1 quart molasses
$\frac{3}{4}$ pound chopped onions

FOR AN ARMY OF 10
RATIONS: 1 $\frac{1}{4}$ pounds dried lima beans
Water
2 pounds cooked, sliced ham
1 teaspoon salt
Dash pepper
$\frac{1}{3}$ cup molasses or brown sugar
$\frac{1}{3}$ cup chopped onions

ORDERS: Wash lima beans. Add just enough water to cover; soak for 30 minutes. Heat beans, to boiling, in the water in which they were soaked; reduce heat and simmer until almost tender, being careful that the skins are not broken. Add cooked ham, molasses, onions, salt, and pepper; mix well. Place mixture in a greased baking pan. Bake in slow oven (325°) for 45 minutes to an hour.

A few extra olives go well with just about anything. New Year's Day 1951, somewhere in Korea.

LOBSTER NEWBURG
KOREAN WAR

Despite general agreement that the pun is the lowest form of humor, we are going to serve up a lobster tale (Sorry). Lobster Newburg dates from the 1800s and the famously posh Delmonico's Restaurant in New York City. Catering to the very famous, the very fashionable, and the very rich, Delmonico's was known for its service as well as its cuisine.

The story is that chef Charles Ranhofer was asked to prepare this dish for shipping magnate Ben Wenberg. Wenberg had been served a similar dish while on a trip to South America. Ranhofer complied and named the dish Lobster Wenberg in honor of his patron. Things took a turn, however, when Wenberg, after a brawl in the restaurant, was banned from Delmonico's. Not only was Ben banned, so was his name. The dish, however, was much more popular than was Wenberg, so it remained on the menu, rechristened "Lobster Newburg."

FOR AN ARMY OF 100

RATIONS: 15 pounds lobster
    meat
1 pint butter
$\frac{1}{4}$ quart sifted flour
2 gallons cream
48 egg yolks
1 tablespoon salt
Dash cayenne pepper
1 pint lemon juice
Dash paprika
100 slices toast

FOR AN ARMY OF 10

RATIONS: 1 $\frac{1}{2}$ pounds lobster
    meat
$\frac{1}{4}$ cup butter
1 $\frac{1}{2}$ tablespoons flour
3 cups cream
5 egg yolks
$\frac{1}{4}$ teaspoon salt
Dash cayenne pepper
3 tablespoons lemon
    juice
Dash paprika
10 slices toast

ORDERS: Cut lobster meat into cubes and cook in melted butter for 5 minutes. Add flour. Gradually add cream and bring mixture slowly to boiling point. Let simmer gently for 2 or 3 minutes. Add well-beaten egg yolks, salt, and cayenne and cook over very low heat for 2 minutes longer. Add lemon juice and remove from heat. Serve on toast. Garnish with paprika.

MILK TOAST
WORLD WAR I

Milk toast is a soft, bland mush that was a popular breakfast food for the infirm and ailing. For military purposes, it was a hot dish that was easily prepared even when the larders were running low. The bread was filling, the sugar provided energy, and the milk was full of calcium and vitamins. Even so, the name is not really a great morale-builder, particularly for the warrior class, and this recipe disappeared from military cookery following the Great War.

FOR AN ARMY OF 100
RATIONS: 12 pounds bread
2 pounds sugar
Milk to cover

FOR AN ARMY OF 10
RATIONS: 20 slices bread
$^3/_4$ cup sugar
6 cups milk

ORDERS: Slices of bread left over may be used. Place in a large bake pan not more than 1/3 full, and brown in a 15 count oven (325°).* Saturate with boiling water and sprinkle with sugar. Serve in vegetable dishes, with milk poured over it.

*See Temperature Gauge, Hand-Type, page 150.

OATMEAL MUSH
WORLD WAR I

Like its counterpart, corn meal mush, this hot breakfast cereal was a mainstay of the breakfast mess through several wars and conflicts. This recipe, from years before instant and quick-cooking oats, requires a longer cooking time.

FOR AN ARMY OF 60
RATIONS: 5 pounds oatmeal
$^1/_2$ pound sugar
1 ounce salt
6 cans evaporated milk
3 $^1/_2$ gallons water

FOR AN ARMY OF 6
RATIONS: 1 cup oatmeal (not instant or quick-cooking)
2 $^1/_4$ teaspoons sugar
1 teaspoon salt
1 $^1/_4$ cups milk
5 $^1/_4$ cups water

ORDERS: Place the water in a boiler and allow it to come to a boil; whip the oatmeal in, slowly adding salt and sugar, and boil for 5 minutes. Let simmer 1/2 hour and serve with milk and sugar.

OATMEAL

PINEAPPLE CHICKEN
VIETNAM WAR

Originally introduced to the military mess during the Vietnam War, this casserole is still popular (appearing as the daily bill of fare of at least two Air Force enlisted men's menus in the fall of 2005).

This casserole is a wonderful blend of chicken and fruit. The acidity of the pineapple helps to tenderize the chicken. Usually served with rice, this dish is great for a crowd.

FOR AN ARMY OF 100

RATIONS: 50 pounds chicken,
broiler-fryer, cut up
2 tablespoons mono-
sodium glutamate
1 cup soy sauce
$\frac{1}{2}$ cup salt
$\frac{1}{2}$ cup sugar
2 quarts flour
1 cup soy sauce
3 quarts (1 No. 10 can)
crushed pineapple

FOR AN ARMY OF 10

RATIONS: 5 pounds chicken,
broiler-fryer, cut up
Dash monosodium
glutamate (if desired)
2 tablespoons soy
sauce
2 $\frac{1}{4}$ teaspoons salt
2 $\frac{1}{4}$ teaspoons sugar
$\frac{3}{4}$ cup flour
1 $\frac{1}{4}$ cups canned
crushed pineapple

ORDERS: Wash chicken thoroughly under running water. Drain well. Sprinkle cut side of chickens with monosodium glutamate. Combine soy sauce, salt, and sugar. Spread on chicken pieces. Dredge chicken in flour. Fry 10 minutes. Place chicken, skin side up, in pans. Combine soy sauce and pineapple; spread evenly over chicken. Cover pan. Bake 1 1/4 hours at 300° or until chicken is tender.

U.S. Special Forces hat,
Vietnam

ORIENTAL TUNA PATTIES
OPERATION IRAQI FREEDOM

Never let it be said that our boys aren't up for a little adventure. They'll have one with this recipe.

Tuna burgers have now climbed to a whole new level. Gone are the days of that fishy tuna smell in the chow line. The sweet and sour taste and the salty crunch of a peanut put a little zing into this delicious meal.

FOR AN ARMY OF 100

RATIONS: 1 quart plus 2 cups water
1 $\frac{1}{2}$ cups soy sauce
1 $\frac{1}{2}$ cups lime juice
$\frac{3}{4}$ cup brown sugar, packed
2 tablespoons garlic powder
2 tablespoons ground ginger
$\frac{1}{8}$ teaspoon red pepper
2 cups water
1 cup cornstarch
2 $\frac{1}{4}$ cups sliced green onions
1 $\frac{1}{2}$ cups shelled peanuts
15 $\frac{3}{8}$ pounds canned tuna
1 gallon plus 2 $\frac{1}{2}$ quarts bread crumbs
2 quarts whole, frozen eggs
2 quarts plus $\frac{1}{2}$ cup chopped onions
2 quarts plus 2 $\frac{1}{8}$ cups chopped celery
$\frac{3}{4}$ cup plus 2 table-spoons prepared horseradish
$\frac{1}{2}$ cup plus 3 table-spoons minced garlic
$\frac{1}{4}$ cup plus $\frac{1}{3}$ table-spoon nonstick cooking spray

FOR AN ARMY OF 10

RATIONS: 1 cup water
$\frac{1}{2}$ cup soy sauce
$\frac{1}{2}$ cup lime juice
3 $\frac{1}{2}$ teaspoons brown sugar
$\frac{1}{2}$ teaspoon garlic powder
$\frac{1}{2}$ teaspoon ground ginger
Dash red pepper
2 tablespoons water
1 tablespoon cornstarch
$\frac{1}{2}$ cup green onions
$\frac{1}{4}$ cup shelled peanuts
1 $\frac{1}{2}$ pounds canned tuna, packed in water and drained.
2 $\frac{1}{2}$ cups bread crumbs
3 eggs
$\frac{3}{4}$ cup chopped onion
1 cup chopped celery
1 tablespoon prepared horseradish
3 teaspoons minced garlic
Nonstick cooking spray

ORDERS: Combine water, soy sauce, lime juice, brown sugar, garlic powder, ginger, and red pepper. Bring to a boil. Reduce heat. Combine water and cornstarch. Blend until smooth. Add to sauce mixture while stirring. Simmer 3 minutes or until thickened. Add green onions and peanuts. Stir well. Drain tuna; place drained tuna in a mixer bowl. Flake tuna on low speed about 30 seconds or until tuna chunks begin to flake. Add bread crumbs, eggs, onions, celery, horseradish, and garlic. Mix 2 minutes at low speed or until ingredients are combined. Do not overmix. Shape into 4 3/4-ounce patties; place balls on sheet pans. Cover with parchment paper; flatten into patties by pressing down with another sheet pan to a thickness of 1/2 inch. Grill patties on a lightly sprayed 350° griddle 4 to 6 minutes per side or until golden brown. Patties may also be baked in a 400° degree oven for 20–30 minutes or until internal temperature reaches 145°.

K.P. continued even under Operation Desert Shield in 1991. It never ends.

SALMON CAKES
KOREAN WAR

This traditional salmon cake recipe was served with a tomato sauce, although tartar sauce was also popular. Canned salmon was part of the base ration as well as garrison rations and is a good source of protein. Hungry GIs were allotted two salmon cakes per meal and all the sauce they could fit on their plate.

FOR AN ARMY OF 100

RATIONS: 20 pounds canned salmon
7 $\frac{1}{2}$ quarts mashed potatoes, without seasonings
16 eggs
2 $\frac{3}{4}$ quarts bread or cracker crumbs
6 tablespoons salt
Black pepper to taste
Cayenne pepper to taste
1 quart fat (for frying)
1 $\frac{1}{2}$ cups chopped onions
1 pound green peppers

FOR AN ARMY OF 10

RATIONS: 2 pounds canned salmon
3 cups mashed potatoes, without seasonings
2 eggs
$\frac{1}{2}$ cup bread or cracker crumbs
1 $\frac{1}{4}$ teaspoons salt
Black pepper to taste
Cayenne pepper to taste
$\frac{1}{3}$ cup fat (for frying)
$\frac{1}{3}$ cup onions
3 tablespoons green pepper

ORDERS: Remove skin from salmon. Combine salmon, salmon liquid, potatoes, eggs, crumbs, salt, pepper, onions, and cayenne. Make into cakes weighing 3 ounces (3 inches in diameter, 1 inch thick). Fry in fat until brown.

January 1951 in Korea, and these guys are cold as they line up for breakfast before heading out. During winter, troops were served four full meals a day because their bodies needed all the fuel they could get.

SALT PORK AND HARD BREAD
CIVIL WAR

Military cookery was neither art nor science during the Civil War, particularly for the enlisted men on both sides of the conflict. It was all pretty much improvised.

There were no formal military cooking schools at the onset of the war. Rations were distributed and the men typically arranged themselves into mess units of six or eight. It was all rather informal. If one of your messmates had been a cook before the war, you were uncommonly lucky. Usually, everyone just took turns. Recipes were developed on the spot, as the designated cook hunched over the skillet. No doubt, more than a few suggestions—good-natured and otherwise—added a little spice to the proceedings. Before too long, a mess crew had a pretty good idea of whom they would, and would not, designate as the evening's cook.

Salt pork was a standard ration. The pork would be salted as a preservative and shipped in a brine. Like hardtack, it had to be soaked in fresh water to come anywhere near to being palatable.

These are two traditional trial-and-error recipes. Frankly, they taste about the same. The main difference lies in final presentation.

RATIONS: Meat   Hard bread
         Onions   Parsley
         Pepper   Water

Method One: Soak the hard bread in cold water for 1 hour. Wash, clean, and boil the pork. Drain the water off the hard bread, and cut up the pork into thin slices. Peel and slice the onions, wash and chop up the parsley. Pour a little water into the camp kettle; place a layer of the slices of pork at the bottom of the kettle, with some onions, parsley, and pepper, then a layer of the soaked hard bread on top, then another layer of pork, and so on alternately, until the kettle is nearly full. Cover the whole with water and cook gently over a slow fire for 1 hour and 15 minutes and serve.

Method Two: Treat the pork, onions, parsley, as above. Soak the hard bread for two hours, then squeeze it dry. Mince up the pork and mix it with the hard bread, onions, parsley, and pepper; then roll it into balls and place them in a camp kettle with sufficient water to cover, and cook gently over a slow fire for 1 hour, and serve.

These recipes can also be prepared in the camp kettle lids, by placing the layers of pork and hard bread or balls in one camp kettle lid, covering it with another, and placing a few live embers underneath and on top of the lids.

SCOTCH WOODCOCK
VIETNAM WAR

This recipe comes with a disclaimer, to wit: Following this recipe to the letter will not result in an authentic Scotch woodcock. Rather, if you follow this recipe to the letter, you will get the American military's version of an authentic Scotch woodcock. It's not bad, but it is not authentic.

Authentic-from-Scotland Scotch woodcock calls for, nay requires, anchovy fillets. Unfortunately, not many military cooks had anchovy fillets or anchovy paste or anything anchovy on their requisition lists. So this was the best that could be done under the circumstances. The military likes to think this recipe retains the spirit, if not the aquatic flavor, of the original Scottish dish.

FOR AN ARMY OF 100

RATIONS: 1 $\frac{3}{4}$ quarts nonfat dry milk

9 $\frac{1}{3}$ quarts warm water

3 $\frac{3}{4}$ cups butter or margarine, melted

1 $\frac{1}{2}$ quarts sifted flour

4 $\frac{1}{2}$ tablespoons salt

3 pounds 12 ounces grated or shredded cheddar cheese

144 hard-cooked eggs, sliced

2 cups bread crumbs

$\frac{1}{2}$ cup butter or margarine, melted

FOR AN ARMY OF 10

RATIONS: $\frac{3}{4}$ cup nonfat dry milk

2 $\frac{1}{2}$ cups warm water

$\frac{1}{3}$ cup butter or margarine, melted

$\frac{2}{3}$ cup sifted flour

1 teaspoon salt

$\frac{1}{4}$ cup grated or shredded cheddar cheese

14 hard-cooked eggs, sliced

3 $\frac{1}{2}$ tablespoons bread crumbs

2 $\frac{1}{4}$ teaspoons butter or margarine, melted

ORDERS: Reconstitute milk; heat to just below boiling. DO NOT BOIL. Blend butter or margarine, flour, and salt together; stir until smooth. Add roux to milk, stirring constantly. Heat 5 to 10 minutes until thickened. Stir as necessary. Add cheese. Stir until cheese is melted and sauce is smooth. Add eggs to sauce. Mix lightly. Combine bread crumbs and butter or margarine. Sprinkle mixture over eggs. Bake at 325° for 20 minutes or until crumbs are browned.

SLANG

Midrats
(Navy; contemporary): A contraction of "midnight rations." This is a meal served in the crew's mess at midnight for those standing overnight watch. Usually it's just leftovers that have been reheated.

SHRIMP CREOLE WITH RICE
KOREAN WAR

Creole cooking originated in New Orleans and surroundings early in the eighteenth century. A most happy blending of European, Native American, and African influences, Creole cuisine incorporates the refined tastes of the aristocrats with the new foods available in America.

Traditional Creole is hot and spicy, and you know you've been there when you've had it. The military version doesn't have quite the same kick, since it is an acquired taste (and not everyone wants to make the acquisition).

Shrimp Creole, along with gumbo, are two of the most famous Creole dishes.

FOR AN ARMY OF 100

RATIONS: 25 pounds raw shrimp
2 quarts chopped onions
1 pound chopped celery
1 pound chopped green pepper
1 pound fat
$1/2$ pint sifted flour
8 quarts canned tomatoes
7 tablespoons salt
5 tablespoons Worcestershire sauce
3 quarts uncooked rice

FOR AN ARMY OF 10

RATIONS: $2 1/2$ pounds shrimp
$2/3$ cup onions
$1/3$ cup celery
$1/3$ cup green pepper
3 tablespoons fat
$1 1/2$ tablespoons flour
3 cups tomatoes
2 teaspoons salt
$1 1/2$ teaspoons Worcestershire sauce
$1 1/4$ cups uncooked rice

ORDERS: Cover shrimp with boiling water, salted. Cook 15 minutes. Drain. Plunge into cold water to cool quickly. Remove shell. Remove black vein with sharp, pointed knife. Fry onions, celery, and green pepper in melted fat until golden brown. Add flour and tomatoes and cook until smooth and slightly thick. Add shrimp and seasoning and heat. Cook rice and drain. Serve over rice.

SLOW ROASTED RABBIT
WAR OF 1812

As a country, we weren't quite ready for the War of 1812, either politically or militarily.

Like many wars, this one was divisive. Indeed, after the war had begun, it had so little support that the states of New England sent representatives to an extraordinary convention in Hartford to consider the question of seceding from the Union.

From the military standpoint, we were in really bad shape. Our small professional standing army was scattered across a very large area. The majority of our fighting forces were state militias, unprofessional and undisciplined, but with a spirit inspired, at least in part, by the necessity of protecting kith and kin.

Supplies for troops in the field were sketchy, at best. But, for many, that was of little import. These were self-reliant folk, and most knew their way around a campfire. It was an age when "What's for dinner?" was answered by "What did you catch today?"

This is a traditional recipe, born of the woodman's craft and hard experience gained by a lone hunter working old-growth forests in an ongoing effort to feed his family.

ORDERS: Make a slow fire of medium to hot coals. Find a green sapling and remove small branches and leaves to create a spit. Skin and clean the rabbit and remove the head. Affix rabbit to the sapling by tying the front and back paws to the sapling. Season rabbit with salt and herbs. Place rabbit over coals, taking care not to get it too close to burn. Cook slowly, turning over the coals, for several hours. Cook rabbit thoroughly.

A typical field kitchen of the Mexican War. It wasn't quite every man for himself, but it wasn't far from it. The army cooks prepared dinner in the field over camp fires and rudimental cook stoves.

SLUMGULLION
WORLD WAR I

Every major conflict produces its own lore. There is slang unique unto the time and circumstances. There are tales to be told of little glories and of magnificent failures. Great sweeping movements of troops and matériel. Generals and politicians and great men of noble sentiment.

Then there are the guys in the field who are ones pulling the triggers and ducking the shells (and the officers). Improvisation often born of desperation.

Such is the story of slumgullion. It was never codified in official military cookery, but every doughboy in the trenches knew it well. They called it "slum," and it was an improvised stew made of some of this and a little bit of that. It was often watered-down and runny. But it was hot, and it was filling. And there were times when that was all you really needed.

RATIONS: 2 pounds stew beef
4 onions, sliced
2 large cans tomatoes
$1/3$ cup flour
1 teaspoon poultry
seasoning or salt
and pepper to taste

ORDERS: Cut meat into 1-inch cubes and place in a large pot or casserole. Cover with the onions and sprinkle with salt. Pour tomatoes over onions and meat, and salt again. Add poultry seasoning or pepper. Cover pan and bake slowly (about 275°) for several hours. While stew is cooking, combine flour with 1/2 cup cold water and set aside. When meat is cooked, stir in the flour and water to thicken the stew. Serve with mashed potatoes or noodles.

"How to Eat Slum with a Bayonet" — Army humor after World War I exhibited bayonet etiquette and the gap between officers and men.

SHAD

General George E. Pickett

General Fitzhugh Lee

General George Pickett (1825–75), and General Fitzhugh Lee (1835–1905), were both brave Confederate commanders, veterans of combat in the War Between the States, fiercely loyal to the Confederacy, and considered by many to be heroes of "The Lost Cause."

But.

In all candor, the best interests of historical accuracy force us to admit that neither of these guys will ever be accused of being the brightest crayon in the box.

Pickett will forever be linked with that disastrous charge (it wasn't his fault) at Gettysburg. He was a good soldier, despite graduating from West Point absolutely last in the class of 1846. As his commanding officer, James Longstreet, supposedly remarked, "That was quite a feat, considering his classmates."

Lee, nephew of General Robert E. Lee, also had his difficulties at West Point. He graduated in the class of 1856, forty-fifth in a class of forty-nine. So it comes as no real surprise that these two

This Confederate artillery battery in the defensive works of Petersburg, Virginia, is pictured just after falling to Union forces during the 1865 siege.

teamed up to produce one of the largest debacles (on the Confederate side) of the Civil War.

It was spring 1865, in the waning days of the war, and Pickett had been sent with a force of 10,000 to defend the vital railroad junction at Five Forks, just outside Petersburg, Virginia. Federal general Phil Sheridan was threatening Five Forks. If he broke through and took the junction, the rear of the Confederate Army of Northern Virginia would be endangered.

Pickett sent his cavalry commander, Fitzhugh Lee, to attack Sheridan, but finding the enemy in greater strength than anticipated, Fitz Lee pulled back. By now, Pickett's command was isolated from the main body of the Confederate army. He wired to General Robert E. Lee for reinforcements.

These were hard days for the Confederacy. Lee's army had been besieged in Petersburg for nearly a year. Supplies were low; there was almost no food. The junction at Five Forks was Petersburg's sole lifeline, and without it, the Confederacy would surely fall. Lee wired back to hold Five Forks at all costs.

Pickett's command was starving, outnumbered, and nearly surrounded. It was a desperate situation.

As luck would have it, one of Pickett's generals—Thomas Rosser—was an avid fisherman, and he had discovered the shad were running in the creek. So, apparently acting on the saying, "A bad day of fishing is better than a good day fighting Phil Sheridan," he had gone out and caught himself a mess of fish. He invited the other two generals over to his camp, about ten miles from the main body of troops, and they had themselves a big old fish-fry.

One problem with this was that neither Pickett nor Fitz Lee had bothered to tell anyone where they were going. Another problem was that their going left General Rooney Lee (son of Robert E.) as senior officer in the field and, thus, in command; but Rooney didn't know it. The biggest problem of all was that just as the generals sat down to eat, Sheridan attacked with 40,000 men and pretty much ran over the Confederates at Five Forks.

By the time George Pickett and Fitz Lee found out what was happening, it was all over. The operative word being "all": the Battle of Five Forks, the Army of Northern Virginia, and the Confederacy.

Five Forks wasn't the last battle of the war, but it certainly led the way to the last battle. Because of this rail junction being lost, Petersburg was no longer defensible, and Robert E. Lee had to abandon its fortifications and try for the next major rail junction, a little town called Appomattox.

"Pass the tartar sauce, please. By the way, did you hear something over on the right, General?"

STEW EL RANCHO
WORLD WAR I

The early manuals for military cooks were not as detailed as recipes in use today. Techniques and seasonings were often merely suggested, or assumed, by the writer.

In this recipe, we see both a detailed method of slicing and preparing the vegetables, and the casual mention of spices and seasonings, without measurements. Some of the spices, by the way, will not be found in today's typical kitchen spice rack. Chili colorado is another term for dried red chili pods. Comina or comino is now commonly referred to as cumin and is prevalent in chili recipes.

FOR AN ARMY OF 100

RATIONS: 12 pounds meat; cut in
1 $\frac{1}{2}$-inch cubes
10 pounds potatoes
2 cans tomatoes
3 pounds carrots
4 pounds turnips
4 pounds cabbage,
with core in
3 pounds small onions

FOR AN ARMY OF 10

RATIONS: 1 $\frac{1}{4}$ pounds stew meat
2 cups potatoes
$\frac{1}{3}$ cup tomatoes
$\frac{2}{3}$ cup carrots,
quartered
$\frac{3}{4}$ cup turnips, sliced
$\frac{3}{4}$ cup cabbage, sliced
$\frac{2}{3}$ cup pearl onions

ORDERS: Place the meat and such vegetables as turnips, carrots, and tomatoes in a large pan of cold water and bring slowly to a boil. Let simmer until the meat is tender and then add the remaining vegetables, season with salt chili colorado, comina, and oregano, and cook until done. All ingredients should be thoroughly cooked but not broken into pieces in the cooking. The liquid should cover all the solids by about 1 inch. It should not be pasty, but of the nature of broth gravy, and have a reddish hue from the chili pepper and tomatoes. The stew is improved by a bunch of parsley chopped fine and added just before serving, and a few sprigs of parsley may be used for garnishing. Serve hot with vegetables whole as far as possible. Any fresh meat and any vegetable may be used for this stew.

SWEET AND SOUR FRANKFURTERS
VIETNAM WAR

They are not hot dogs. Never hot dogs. They are Frankfurters. Sometimes Frankfurter Sausage. Vienna Sausage during World War I. But at least they are not "steak, tube-type."

Our soldiers, at least officially, have carried on a love affair with frankfurters since World War II. And there have been nearly 100 different ways of preparing and serving them, from the lowly "—and Beans" included in the first C-rations, to some rather exotic twists.

This Vietnam-era variation introduces some spice and creativity. Perfect for a field mess or a Sunday ball game.

FOR AN ARMY OF 100

RATIONS: 1 $\frac{1}{2}$ cups dehydrated onion soup
1 $\frac{1}{2}$ gallons boiling water
1 $\frac{1}{2}$ quarts sweet cucumber pickles, finely chopped
$\frac{1}{2}$ cup prepared mustard
1 $\frac{1}{2}$ cups lemon juice
1 $\frac{1}{2}$ cups brown sugar
$\frac{3}{4}$ cup cornstarch
2 cups cold water
12 22-ounce cans frankfurters

FOR AN ARMY OF 10

RATIONS: 2 tablespoons dehydrated onion soup mix
2 cups boiling water
$\frac{2}{3}$ cup sweet cucumber pickles, finely chopped
2 $\frac{1}{4}$ teaspoons prepared mustard
2 tablespoons lemon juice
2 tablespoons brown sugar
3 $\frac{1}{2}$ teaspoons cornstarch
3 $\frac{1}{2}$ tablespoons cold water
1 $\frac{1}{2}$ pounds frankfurters

ORDERS: Add soup mix to water; cover and simmer 10 minutes. Add pickles, mustard, lemon juice, and sugar. Stir until sugar is dissolved, bring to a boil. Combine cornstarch and water to make a smooth paste; add to mixture, stirring constantly. Cook 10 minutes or until clear and thickened. Add frankfurters to sauce; simmer 10 minutes.

Candied Sweet Potatoes
Baked Beans
Baked Peas
Banana Salad
Baked Crispy Peaches
Bavarian Cabbage
Beets in Orange Lemon Sauce
Caronip Patties
Cauliflower au Gratin
Cider Applesauce
Club Spinach
Cranberry Apple Relish
Creamed Cabbage
Creamed Potatoes
French Fried Tomatoes
German Boiled Potatoes
Hacienda Potatoes
Hot Potato Salad
Savory Green Beans
Spiced Fruit Cup
Sugared Parsnips
Vegetable Stew

CHAPTER 4
FRUITS & VEGETABLES

CANDIED SWEET POTATOES
WORLD WAR I

It seems that sweet potatoes only find their way to the family table these days during Thanksgiving dinner. It was not always so. This vegetable has a long history.

It is believed the sweet potato is native to the Yucatán Peninsula of Mexico and was common throughout Central America by the time Columbus arrived. Indeed, it was one of the exotic foods Columbus brought back to Spain after his first journey.

During the nineteenth century sweet potatoes were common fare. They were often found in the haversacks of soldiers during the Civil War and were one of the primary rations served to Union prisoners held at the infamous Andersonville prison camp in Georgia. African American agricultural chemist George Washington Carver (1860–1943), famous for his work with peanuts, came up with 118 different things to do with a sweet potato.

By the way, sweet potatoes are not yams. A yam is a vegetable native to Africa and the Pacific Islands. Real yams can be real big. (On the island of Ponape in the South Pacific, where they know something about yams, the tubers are defined as "two-man," "four-man," or "six-man," depending on how many guys it takes to lift one. They regularly grow to a hundred pounds or more.)

A hot meal brings a smile to this World War I doughboy. His mess kit was a self-contained unit with both plates and utensils. In a pinch, it could be used as a cooking vessel.

Confusion between sweet potatoes and yams dates from colonial times. The theory goes that slaves, familiar with the African vegetable, began calling sweet potatoes yams because they looked and tasted similar. The state of Louisiana then intensified the misnomer as a marketing ploy. In order to differentiate their sweet potatoes from the ones grown in New England, Louisiana started officially calling them yams. North Carolina and Georgia both thought that this was a pretty good idea and followed suit. The U.S. Department of Agriculture, which cares about such things, stepped in and declared that a sweet potato is, indeed, just a sweet potato and not a yam, and all packaging that says otherwise is misleading and illegal (if not just plain silly). So now when you buy a can of yams, you will note that the label also says it is a can of sweet potatoes. Unless, of course, it really is a can of yams.

Oh, and sweet potatoes aren't a version of those white potatoes that are grown in Idaho either. Could all this confusion be one of the reasons we don't see sweet potatoes outside Thanksgiving? Perhaps. But the military still likes its sweet potatoes. At Thanksgiving in 2004, during Operation Iraqi Freedom, some 25,000 pounds of sweet potatoes were shipped to American forces in the Gulf region.

This recipe was originally published in the *Manual for Army Cooks* (1916).

FOR AN ARMY OF 60

RATIONS: 20 pounds sweet
potatoes
1 pound butter
1 pound sugar
1 pound beef stock,
strained

FOR AN ARMY OF 6

RATIONS: 4 cups sweet potatoes
3 tablespoons butter
3 tablespoons sugar
1 $1/2$ cups beef stock,
strained

ORDERS: Wash the potatoes and boil until fairly well done, peel and slice lengthwise. Spread into three layers in a bake pan, putting about one-third of the sugar and butter on top of each layer. Pour the beef stock over the whole and bake in a medium hot oven (375°) for 40 minutes to 1 hour.

BAKED BEANS
WORLD WAR II

Beans have been a part of military rations since 1775. During the American Revolution, beans were a large part of the daily ration, the standard issue being almost half a pound each day. By the time of the American Civil War, the amount had decreased to just over two and a half ounces per day. As canning processes improved, canned beans became part of the K-ration and standard fare for troops in the field. Hot or cold (usually cold), baked beans provided a "stick-to-your-ribs" meal for the hungry soldier.

FOR AN ARMY 50

RATIONS: 18 pounds beans
4 pounds bacon
1 pint molasses
1 pint catsup
2 ounces dry mustard
2 pounds chopped onions
2 pounds tomatoes

TO FEED 3 TROOPS

RATIONS: 4 $\frac{1}{2}$ cups beans
1 cup bacon
$\frac{1}{4}$ cup molasses
$\frac{1}{4}$ cup catsup
2 teaspoons dry mustard
$\frac{1}{2}$ cup chopped onions
$\frac{1}{2}$ cup tomatoes

There wasn't much time to celebrate holidays on the front lines. This is Christmas Eve, 1944, somewhere in Belgium.

ORDERS: Wash and soak the beans for 4 hours or overnight in cold water. Drain, place in hot water,
and simmer for 2 hours. Drain and place beans in
bake pans or covered earthen crocks. Mix in the
chopped onions and tomatoes. Season to taste
with salt and pepper. Place sliced bacon on top of
the beans. Make a mixture of the molasses, catsup,
and mustard, adding a little vinegar if dry mustard
is used, and pour over the beans. Cover the pan
and bake in a slow oven (below 200°—24 counts*)
for 4 hours or until tender. Serve hot.

In cold weather the soaking may be overnight,
in which case the 2-hour simmering will not be
necessary. In hot weather the beans may sour if
soaked when a cool temperature cannot be
obtained. When this condition is met, beans may
be baked as follows:

Wash the beans in cold water, drain, and place
in cold water; simmer 45 minutes, drain, and put
beans in bake pan. Mix in chopped onions and
tomatoes and season with salt and pepper. Place
sliced bacon on top of the beans. Make a mixture of
the molasses, catsup, and mustard, and pour over
beans. Cover the pan and bake in a slow oven for 5
hours or until tender. Serve hot.

*See page 150.

BAKED PEAS
KOREAN WAR

"Peas! Peas! Peas! Eating goober peas!" This refrain from the American Civil War is familiar to many people (see sidebar).

This recipe does not require peas of the goober variety, but rather the green English pea, which has been part of human diets for many thousands of years. Peas have been found in the tombs of ancient Troy, and, because they are "easy keepers," were part of the foodstuffs brought to America by the first English colonists.

FOR AN ARMY OF 100

RATIONS: 40 pounds peas
Salt
Water
1 No. 10 can tomatoes
3 to 5 pounds flour
1 $\frac{1}{2}$ pints chopped
green pepper
1 cup chopped onions
4 tablespoons chopped
pimientos
8 tablespoons brown
sugar
3 tablespoons salt
4 tablespoons melted
butter
1 $\frac{1}{4}$ quarts dry bread
crumbs

TO FEED 3 TROOPS

RATIONS: 5 $\frac{1}{3}$ cups peas
Salt
Water
1 $\frac{1}{3}$ cups tomatoes
4 $\frac{1}{2}$ cups flour
$\frac{1}{4}$ cup chopped green
pepper
1 $\frac{1}{2}$ tablespoons
onions
1 tablespoon pimiento
2 $\frac{1}{4}$ teaspoons brown
sugar
$\frac{3}{4}$ teaspoon salt
1 teaspoon butter
$\frac{1}{2}$ cup dry bread crumbs

ORDERS: Shell peas (if necessary); wash in cold water. Barely cover peas with boiling salted water. Heat to boiling point; reduce heat and simmer until tender. Drain and reserve liquid. Drain tomatoes and reserve liquid. Combine liquids from peas and tomatoes. Mix flour and a small amount of liquid, using 3 ounces or 12 tablespoons flour (3 1/2 tablespoons) to each quart (cup) liquid measured; stir until smooth. Heat remaining liquid; add flour mixture slowly. Heat to boiling point, boil 2 minutes, stirring constantly. Add peas, tomatoes, green peppers, onions, pimientos, sugar, and salt; mix well.

Pour melted butter over bread crumbs. Pour vegetables into baking pans. Sprinkle with buttered crumbs. Bake in moderate oven (375°) 20 to 30 minutes.

GOOBER PEAS

Sitting by the roadside on a summer's day,
Chatting with my mess-mates, passing time away,
Lying in the shadows underneath the trees,
Goodness, how delicious, eating goober peas.

Chorus: Peas, peas, peas, peas,
Eating goober peas.
Goodness, how delicious,
Eating goober peas.

When a horse-man passes, the soldiers have a rule,
To cry out their loudest, "Mister, here's your mule!"
But another custom, enchanting-er than these
Is wearing out your grinder, eating goober peas.

(Chorus)

Just before the battle, the General hears a row.
He says, "The Yanks are coming, I hear their rifles now."
He looks down the roadway, and what d'ya think he sees?
The Georgia Militia cracking goober peas.

(Chorus)

I think my song has lasted just about enough,
The subject's interesting, but the rhymes are mighty rough.
I wish the war was over, so free from rags and fleas,
We'd kiss our wives and sweethearts, say good-bye to
    goober peas.

—Traditional; camp song of the Confederate army during the
Civil War (1861–65)

Goober: a peanut. A corrupted form of the Bantu word *nguba*,
this is one of the few Americanisms that can be traced, via the
slave trade, to Africa.

Various usages from the Civil War include:
Goobers—Troops from Georgia
Goober digger—A backwoodsman
Goober grabber—A Georgian
Worth a goober—Something that amounts to a lot

BANANA SALAD
VIETNAM WAR

Bananas began to be a regular part of military rations when American forces were in Korea. Advances in refrigerated transportation as well as coordinated supply lines allowed more fresh fruits and vegetables to become part of the military diet. This recipe, from the Vietnam era, was often served as a first course but can also be a light dessert.

FOR AN ARMY OF 100

RATIONS: 50 bananas
$^3/_4$ cup nonfat dry milk
1 $^3/_4$ cups warm water
1 $^1/_2$ quarts salad dressing
3 quarts shredded, sweetened coconut
4 pounds lettuce

FOR AN ARMY OF 10

RATIONS: 5 bananas
3 $^1/_2$ teaspoons nonfat dry milk
3 tablespoons warm water
$^2/_3$ cup salad dressing
1 $^1/_4$ cups shredded sweetened coconut
Lettuce for serving

ORDERS: Cut bananas in half crosswise; set aside. Reconstitute milk; add to dressing. Blend well. Dip each banana half into dressing mixture. Roll bananas in coconut. Place each coated banana-half on a lettuce leaf.

BAKED CRISPY PEACHES
KOREAN WAR

This is a quick and easy treat that can be served as a side dish or dessert. Dress it up with a scoop of vanilla ice cream for the perfect ending to a meal.

FOR AN ARMY OF 100

RATIONS: 3 No. 10 cans peach halves
2 pounds brown sugar
$^1/_8$ pound butter
2 pounds cornflakes

TO FEED 3 TROOPS

RATIONS: 4 cups peach halves
$^2/_3$ cup brown sugar
$^1/_4$ cup butter
3 cups cornflakes

ORDERS: Place peach halves, hollow side up, in a greased or nonstick baking pan. Fill centers with brown sugar, dot with butter, and sprinkle with cornflakes. Pour juice around peaches. Bake in a moderate oven (375°) about 25 minutes. Serve warm.

BAVARIAN CABBAGE
WORLD WAR I

Cabbage had many attractions for the military cook. It keeps well and has many nutrients essential to good health. This recipe, easily made from staple items, is similar to sauerkraut, which is not boiled, but soaked in brine for several weeks. Using cider vinegar will give this dish a touch of sweetness.

During the Great War, as World War I was called, sauerkraut became known as "freedom cabbage." It makes you think of the "freedom fries" and "freedom roast coffee" of a later era.

FOR AN ARMY OF 100
RATIONS: 30 pounds cabbage
5 pounds salt pork or sliced bacon
1 quart vinegar

FOR AN ARMY OF 10
RATIONS: 3 pounds cabbage (about 6 cups)
1 cup bacon or salt pork
$\frac{1}{3}$ cup vinegar

ORDERS: Strip off the outer leaves and cut out the cores of the cabbage; cut up as for sauerkraut; wash and place in a boiler; add the salt pork (or bacon), vinegar, and a gallon of water; season with salt and pepper; boil slowly in an open boiler for 3 hours, adding boiling water if necessary; then thicken slightly with a flour batter and boil about 5 minutes longer, when it will be ready to serve.

BEETS IN ORANGE LEMON SAUCE
OPERATION IRAQI FREEDOM

This contemporary military recipe has no cholesterol, a plus in today's health-conscious diets. Beets are also a good source of calcium. The citrus flavors go well with the beets, and it makes an elegant dish for your table.

FOR AN ARMY OF 100

RATIONS: 4 gallons plus two quarts canned beets, including liquid
1 tablespoon ground cloves
1 $\frac{1}{2}$ cups cornstarch
3 cups cold water
3 $\frac{3}{8}$ cups sugar
1 tablespoon salt
$\frac{3}{4}$ cup lemon juice
3 tablespoons lemon rind, grated
3 cups orange juice
1 cup margarine

FOR AN ARMY OF 10

RATIONS: 6 $\frac{1}{2}$ cups canned beets, including liquid
$\frac{1}{4}$ teaspoon ground cloves
2 tablespoons cornstarch
4 tablespoons water
3 tablespoons sugar
$\frac{1}{4}$ teaspoon salt
3 $\frac{1}{2}$ teaspoons lemon juice
$\frac{3}{4}$ teaspoon lemon rind, grated
$\frac{1}{3}$ cup orange juice
$\frac{1}{3}$ cup margarine

ORDERS: Drain beets; reserve liquid. Combine water and reserved liquid in a large saucepan. Add cloves; bring to a boil. Dissolve cornstarch in cold water; add to boiling liquid. Cook 5 minutes, stirring constantly until thick and clear. Add sugar, salt, lemon and orange juices, lemon rind, and margarine to thickened mixture; stir until blended. Add drained beets to sauce. Heat thoroughly.

A chow line in Kuwait during Operation Iraqi Freedom. A hot meal is always a welcome departure from MREs.

CARONIP PATTIES
KOREAN WAR

You would think that just serving a dish made with both turnips and carrots would be enough to strike fear into the heart of a four-year-old toddler (not to mention a twenty-year-old warrior). But that wasn't enough. They had to come up with this name for the concoction. No doubt that put a spring into the step of the guys as they read the mess hall menu.

But surprisingly, these patties are actually a pretty tasty, if unusual, vegetable dish. Turnips are high in vitamin C, and carrots are a good source of beta-carotene, which our bodies convert to vitamin A. Both are low in calories.

FOR AN ARMY OF 100
RATIONS: 8 pounds carrots
8 pounds turnips
3 pounds onions
20 eggs
Bread crumbs
Salt and pepper to taste
4 14 $\frac{1}{2}$-ounce cans
evaporated milk

FOR AN ARMY OF 10
RATIONS: 1 $\frac{1}{2}$ cups carrots
1 $\frac{1}{2}$ cups turnips
1 $\frac{1}{4}$ cups onions
2 eggs
1 $\frac{1}{4}$ cup bread crumbs
Salt and pepper to taste
$\frac{3}{4}$ cups evaporated milk

ORDERS: Peel the carrots, turnips, and onions. Cut to equal size, boil until tender. Drain well and grind. Add 8 (1) well-beaten eggs to the above and mix. Add bread crumbs gradually and mix thoroughly. Form into patties 1/2 inch thick and 2 1/2 inches wide.

Combine the remaining eggs and milk to form a batter and dip patties first into the batter and then into flour or bread crumbs and place on greased sheet pans. Bake in oven at 350° for approximately 10 minutes or until browned.

NOTE: If variety is desired, instead of dipping patties into batter and flour, as patties are formed place them on sheet pan and sprinkle brown sugar over each patty and bake in oven.

CAULIFLOWER AU GRATIN
KOREAN WAR

"Au gratin" literally means "with gratings," but has come to be any dish prepared with buttered bread crumbs and cheese. Many things can be served "au gratin," and the distinct flavor of the cauliflower blends well with the white sauce and cheese in this recipe.

FOR AN ARMY OF 100

RATIONS: 35 pounds cauliflower
Salt
Boiling water
3 quarts white sauce
2 pounds finely chopped cheese
1 cup melted butter
1 $\frac{1}{2}$ pints dried bread crumbs

FOR AN ARMY OF 10

RATIONS: 3 $\frac{1}{2}$ pounds cauliflower
Salt
Boiling water
1 $\frac{1}{4}$ cups white sauce
$\frac{3}{4}$ cup finely chopped cheese
1 $\frac{1}{2}$ tablespoons melted butter
7 tablespoons dried bread crumbs

ORDERS: Cover cauliflower with cold salted water; soak 30 minutes. Wash heads; remove base of stalks and discard large leaves. Add to boiling salted water. Heat to boiling point; reduce heat and simmer, uncovered, 8 to 10 minutes or until tender. Drain and cool. Break into pieces. Prepare white sauce; add cheese and stir until cheese is melted. Place cauliflower in well-greased baking pan. Pour cheese sauce over cauliflower. Pour melted butter over bread crumbs; cover cauliflower with buttered crumbs. Bake in a moderate oven (350°) 30 minutes.

Soupy, soupy, soupy,
Not a single bean.
Porky, porky, porky,
Not a streak of lean.
Coffee, coffee, coffee,
Not a drop of cream.

—Traditional words of mess call

CIDER APPLESAUCE
CIVIL WAR

More commonly known today as apple butter, this sweet preserve was made in camp rather than on the march, owing to its long cooking time. As in many recipes of this era, measures and cooking times are more open than those of today. When making this recipe in your home kitchen—or in camp—fill your kettle with cider, let it reduce by half, and add enough apples to fill again. Let it stew until thick and flavorful.

> **ORDERS:** Fill a large kettle with 4 quarts apple cider. Boil until quantity is reduced by half. Add enough peeled, cored, and quartered apples to fill. Stew over a fire for 4 hours. Add cinnamon if desired.

The first thing in the morning is drill, then drill, then drill again. Between drills we drill and sometimes we stop to eat a little and have a roll call.
—Pennsylvania recruit during his first months of service

A noncommissioned officers' camp mess in the fall of 1863 featured camp table and chairs, some rugged-looking tableware, and perhaps a bottle of oh-be-joyful or two.

CLUB SPINACH
VIETNAM WAR

Popeye the Sailor Man, the most famous sailor never in the Navy, was known for his affection for canned spinach (he always seemed to have some handy). The green leafy vegetable would immediately put power in his punch and spell trouble for the bad guys. Many popular cartoon characters went to war following the attack on Pearl Harbor in 1941. Indeed, the Disney Studios designed quite a number of emblems for various outfits during the war. But Popeye had a jump on them all. In 1936 he, along with his nemesis, the ruffian Bluto, tried to join the infantry. Happily, it didn't work out, and a "swabby" each remained. In 1948, Popeye was added to the official insignia of VP-6, a naval patrol squadron. So, in tribute to all men who fight to the finish ' cause they eat their spinach...

FOR AN ARMY OF 100
RATIONS: 4 No. 10 cans spinach
(3 gallons)
3 quarts cheddar cheese, shredded
2 $\frac{1}{4}$ quarts cracker crumbs, finely ground
1 cup butter or margarine, melted
3 cups bacon, sliced and cut into 1-inch pieces

FOR AN ARMY OF 10
RATIONS: 4 cans spinach –or–
4 cups frozen spinach, thawed and drained well
1 $\frac{1}{4}$ cups cheddar cheese, shredded
1 cup cracker crumbs, finely ground
1 tablespoon butter or margarine, melted
$\frac{1}{3}$ cup bacon, sliced and cut into 1-inch pieces

ORDERS: Drain spinach; chop coarsely and place in a layer in greased pan(s). Cover spinach with cheese. Combine cracker crumbs with butter or margarine. Sprinkle over cheese. Sprinkle bacon over mixture. Bake 30 minutes in a 325° oven or until bacon is crisp and spinach is thoroughly heated.

An army marches on its stomach.
—Attributed to Napoleon, 1769–1821

CRANBERRY APPLE RELISH
KOREAN WAR

Most Americans associate cranberries with the traditional Thanksgiving meal; however, cranberries also go well with pork or chicken. This relish is easy to prepare and adds a bit of sweetness to a savory menu.

FOR AN ARMY OF 100
RATIONS: 7 oranges
3 lemons
2 $\frac{1}{2}$ pounds apples
3 $\frac{1}{2}$ pounds cranberries
4 pounds sugar

FOR AN ARMY OF 100
RATIONS: 1 orange
$\frac{1}{2}$ lemon
$\frac{2}{3}$ cup apples
1 $\frac{1}{2}$ cups cranberries
$\frac{1}{2}$ cup sugar

ORDERS: Wash oranges and lemons, remove peel, and cut into quarters. Remove seeds. Chop pulp. Wash apples; remove seeds and cores. Cut into quarters; chop. Wash cranberries; chop. Combine chopped oranges, lemons, apples, and cranberries. Add sugar; mix well. Refrigerate a few hours before serving.

Stars and Stripes and K-rations. At least the news isn't as old as the rations for these GIs during the Korean War!

CREAMED CABBAGE
VIETNAM WAR

Cabbage is a good source of vitamins C and A and will keep for a week or more if refrigerated. Creamed cabbage is popular in many European cultures. There are recipes claiming Norway, Great Britain, Germany, Poland, and Italy as their originators. Perhaps that is why the military included this hot, comforting dish on its menus. It is something many soldiers would remember from home.

FOR AN ARMY OF 100

RATIONS: 8 gallons fresh cabbage, coarsely shredded
3 tablespoons salt
1 $\frac{1}{2}$ gallons boiling water
2 $\frac{7}{8}$ cups nonfat dry milk
3 $\frac{3}{4}$ quarts warm water
2 cups butter or magarine, melted
2 cups flour
2 tablespoons salt

FOR AN ARMY OF 10

RATIONS: 12 cups fresh cabbage, coarsely shredded
$\frac{3}{4}$ teaspoon salt
3 cups boiling water
$\frac{1}{3}$ cup nonfat dry milk
1 $\frac{1}{2}$ cups warm water
2 $\frac{1}{3}$ tablespoons butter or margarine, melted
2 $\frac{1}{3}$ tablespoons flour
$\frac{1}{2}$ teaspoon salt

A sandwich and some potato salad in a Vietnam firebase— simple but welcome food for homesick soldiers

ORDERS: Add cabbage to salted boiling water. Bring to boil; boil gently uncovered, 8 minutes or until cabbage is just tender. Drain, set aside. Reconstitute milk; heat to just below boiling. DO NOT BOIL. Blend together butter or margarine and flour until smooth. Add cold roux (butter and flour) and salt to milk, stirring constantly. Simmer 5 minutes or until thickened. Add cabbage; mix lightly.

CREAMED POTATOES
WORLD WAR I

The instructions for this World War I–era military recipe illustrate one of the big differences in cooking methods between the military kitchen of 1916 and a contemporary family kitchen. Many military stoves then in operation did not have individual "burners" as we see in today's kitchen stovetops. They were closer to restaurant ranges that have a single continuous, flat cooking surface. Placing a large baking pan on the range, as instructed below, would not have presented a problem for the military cook; but it probably wouldn't work in your kitchen today. Using an electric fry pan, which is deeper than most standard fry pans, will work for this recipe.

FOR AN ARMY OF 60
RATIONS: 22 pounds potatoes
1 gallon beef stock
1 can evaporated milk
2 ounces parsley

FOR AN ARMY OF 6
RATIONS: 4 $\frac{1}{2}$ cups potatoes
$\frac{1}{2}$ cup beef stock
3 tablespoons milk
1 teaspoon parsley

ORDERS: Boil the potatoes until well done; peel and slice crosswise; allow the beef stock to come to a boil on the range; thicken with a flour batter and add the evaporated milk; place the potatoes in a bake pan and pour the mixture over them, just enough to cover the potatoes.

Allow to come to a boil and remove from the range immediately. Meanwhile chop the parsley very fine and, before serving, sprinkle evenly over the potatoes.

To doughboys in Bordeaux, France, there were few places more enjoyable than the Red Cross Canteen.

FRENCH FRIED TOMATOES
VIETNAM WAR

When making this classic Southern recipe, it is important to use green or underripe tomatoes. Ripe tomatoes will fall apart in your pan! This is a great way to use the last of those late summer tomatoes from your garden.

FOR AN ARMY OF 100

RATIONS: 30 pounds (about 105) fresh green or half-ripe tomatoes
2 1/2 quarts flour
6 tablespoons salt
1 tablespoon pepper
3/4 cup nonfat dry milk
3 3/4 cups water
10 eggs
1 gallon dry bread crumbs

FOR AN ARMY OF 10

RATIONS: 10 green or half-ripe tomatoes
1 cup flour
1 3/4 teaspoons salt
Dash pepper
1 tablespoon nonfat dry milk
1/3 cup water
1 egg
1 1/2 cups bread crumbs

ORDERS: Cut tomatoes into 1/2-inch slices. Combine flour, salt, and pepper. Dredge tomato slices in seasoned flour. Reconstitute milk; add egg(s). Dip floured slices in milk-and-egg mixture. Drain. Dredge in bread crumbs; shake off excess crumbs. Fry in 360° oil until golden brown.

The breakfast chow line in Vietnam serves up sausage and eggs. A hot breakfast was satisfying for any soldier in the field.

GERMAN BOILED POTATOES
WORLD WAR II

In Germany, *Salzkartoffeln*, as this dish is known, are heavily salted boiled potatoes. This recipe, from a World War II–era Army cookbook, does not make mention of salt, but the addition of browned onions—and remember most things were browned in bacon fat—places it in the same family of recipes as German potato salad. These potatoes could be served at any meal, equally at home with fried eggs or fried chicken.

FOR AN ARMY OF 100
RATIONS: 30 pounds potatoes
2 pounds onions, browned

FOR AN ARMY OF 10
RATIONS: 3 pounds potatoes
$1/_3$ cup onions, browned

ORDERS: Clean, peel, and cut the potatoes into pieces about the size of an egg, place in cold water, and boil until done. Then place in vegetable dishes and spread about 2 basting spoonfuls of browned onions over the contents of each dish. Serve hot.

Potatoes left over from this recipe may be used in lyonnaise potatoes, salads, fried potatoes, stews, and various other dishes.

Actress Betty Hutton shows how it's done in the mess hall. Hollywood did its share during World War II, stumping for war bonds and making personal appearances—anything to keep up the morale of the troops.

HACIENDA POTATOES
OPERATION IRAQI FREEDOM

The peppers and chili powder give this dish a dash of Tex-Mex and, presumably, the "Hacienda" in the name. These spicy potatoes are good for a hearty breakfast or as an accompaniment to beef or pork.

FOR AN ARMY OF 100

RATIONS: 4 gallons plus 1 $\frac{1}{2}$ quarts potatoes, peeled and cubed
2 gallons water
2 gallons canned tomatoes, drained and diced
1 quart plus 2 cups fresh green peppers, chopped
1 quart plus 2 cups onions, chopped
$\frac{1}{2}$ cup plus 2 $\frac{2}{3}$ tablespoons sugar
1 cup chili powder
$\frac{1}{4}$ cup plus 1 $\frac{2}{3}$ tablespoons salt
$\frac{1}{4}$ cup plus $\frac{1}{3}$ tablespoon garlic powder
2 tablespoons ground cumin
1 tablespoon black pepper
2 cups water
2 cups flour

FOR AN ARMY OF 10

RATIONS: 6 $\frac{1}{2}$ cups potatoes, peeled and cubed
3 cups water
3 cups canned tomatoes, drained and diced
$\frac{2}{3}$ cup fresh green peppers, chopped
$\frac{2}{3}$ cup onions, chopped
3 tablespoons sugar
1 tablespoon chili powder
1 $\frac{1}{4}$ teaspoons salt
1 teaspoon garlic powder
$\frac{1}{2}$ teaspoon cumin
$\frac{1}{4}$ teaspoon black pepper
2 tablespoons water
2 tablespoons flour

ORDERS: Add potatoes to water. Bring to a boil. Reduce heat. Simmer 20 minutes or until potatoes are just tender. Combine tomatoes, green peppers, onions, sugar, chili powder, salt, garlic powder, cumin, and black pepper in a large pot. Bring to a boil, reduce heat, cover and simmer 5 minutes. Blend water and flour to make a smooth paste. Add to sauce. Stir to combine. Simmer 5 minutes or until thickened, stirring occasionally. Add potatoes to sauce. Stir to evenly distribute ingredients. Cover and bring to a boil, stirring occasionally. Uncover and reduce heat. Simmer 10 minutes, stirring occasionally, until potatoes are heated through.

HOT POTATO SALAD
CIVILIAN CONSERVATION CORPS

During the Great Depression, in 1935, nearly 600,000 men were enrolled in the CCC. Most joined for the steady work and reliable paycheck. And although it is not formally documented, there is plenty of anecdotal evidence to suggest quite a few joined just to get the three square meals a day (the money was nice, but the food was vital). Here's what one camp cook chose to feed his crew after a day of felling trees and building roads.

FOR AN ARMY OF 100 CONSERVATIONISTS

RATIONS: 26 pounds potatoes, cooked
36 eggs (hard-cooked)
2 pounds bacon, diced and cooked
4 quarts celery, diced
2 quarts peas, cooked
1 cup pimiento, diced
1 cup parsley, chopped
1 cup onion, chopped
Dressing
5 cups water
5 cups vinegar
2 cups sugar
1 cup bacon fat
$\frac{1}{3}$ cup salt

FOR AN ARMY OF 10 CONSERVATIONISTS

RATIONS: 2 $\frac{1}{2}$ pounds potatoes, cooked
4 eggs (hard-cooked)
$\frac{1}{4}$ pound bacon, diced and cooked
1 $\frac{1}{2}$ cups celery, diced
$\frac{3}{4}$ cup peas, cooked
1 $\frac{1}{2}$ tablespoons pimiento, diced
1 $\frac{1}{2}$ tablespoons parsley, chopped
1 $\frac{1}{2}$ tablespoons onion, chopped
$\frac{3}{4}$ cup water
$\frac{3}{4}$ cup vinegar
9 $\frac{1}{2}$ teaspoons sugar
1 $\frac{1}{2}$ tablespoons bacon fat
1 $\frac{1}{2}$ teaspoons salt

ORDERS: Marinate potatoes in dressing. Mix other ingredients. Put in a steamer and keep hot.

Two of FDR's domestic programs merged in this recruiting poster created by his Works Progress Administration for the Civilian Conservation Corps. At its height in 1935, some 600,000 men were enrolled in the CCC.

JOHN WAYNE

Gather together a fairly representative group of vets—World War II, Korea, or Vietnam—over a cuppa joe, or other situationally appropriate libation, and you'll find them getting all soft and misty-eyed over absent comrades. In the right company, you're likely to hear stories and guffaws about the ladies in this port or just outside that base camp.

And there will probably be at least one who will look you dead in the eye and tell you in all seriousness that he'd never go anywhere without his John Wayne. Odds are that he will then pull out his key ring just to prove that this little marvel of American technology is still carried with pride.

Originally issued in 1942 with the official designation "Opener, Can, Hand, Folding, Type I," they are still an inventory item of the military (NSN 7330-00-242-3506). No one ever calls them that, though; no one ever really did. They're called either a P-38 or a John Wayne.

And they're almost enough to get those guys all misty-eyed.

They really are a marvel of military engineering. More than just military engineering, actually. In the world of industrial design, these things stand out.

Their design is simple, and ideally suited for their primary

A marvel of industrial design: the original P-38, so named because it would open your can of C-rats with just 38 punctures

The big guy in the middle of the second row *is* John Wayne. The other big guys carried *a* John Wayne on their dog tags.

purpose. They are cheap to manufacture. Easy to use. Versatile. Nearly indestructible. They don't rust. They don't break. They don't wear out. They don't pollute. They require no external power source. They're small and lightweight. And they even have a hole, so you can carry them on a chain around your neck with your dog tags or in your pocket on your key ring. In our modern world of ergonomics, it just doesn't get any better than this.

When the Army was working to develop C-rations just prior to the outbreak of World War II, a decision was made to package most of the foodstuffs in small cans. This way the food would be easily transported and would stay fresh for extended periods. (Yes, rations originally packaged for World War II did sometimes wind up being issued during the Korean War; but no, they probably weren't issued yet again in Vietnam. That's just a nasty rumor. At least, that's their story and they are sticking to it.)

The simple truth about putting things in cans, though, is that eventually you would want those things to come out of the cans. The problem was that almost never, particularly when you're out in the field and the muck and the weather, is it convenient to open a can. At least until the NSN 7330-00-242-3506 came along. The Army's Subsistence Research Laboratory was given the task of making the C-rations workable. In one concentrated thirty-day period in the summer of 1942 they did so, by conceiving, refining, designing, and testing the can opener. Some of the best industrial designers in the country worked on that project. And it shows. More than fifty years later, it still hasn't been improved. The same basic design is in use today. You can go to an outdoor store and pick one up for a buck or two, and there's no significant difference between today's civilian version and the original.

Stories of their use, in combat and otherwise, are legion. There's the one about the sergeant in Vietnam who would attack each case of C-rats as they were opened and immediately confiscate every P-38 in the box, just so he could keep track of them and dole them out only as needed. And you will still see stories in the local papers about a veteran who tries to board a flight with one on his key ring. The Department of Homeland Security has been tasked with keeping the country's airlines safe, and DHS just isn't nearly as sentimental as a vet, so they don't like the idea of these things on airplanes. So our vet, who has carried this P-38 in his pocket for several decades now, must choose between giving up his flight and giving up his can opener. The can opener usually loses and goes back to Uncle Sam from whence it came (but at least the guy gets his name in the newspaper when he screams about it).

If we're going to be technically correct here, we should note that there are actually two sizes. The larger is called the John Wayne; the smaller is called the P-38. They came by the names honestly: The original training film demonstrating their use was narrated by John Wayne, and it takes thirty-eight punctures of the can to open the lid.

With the coming of MREs during the 1980s, general distribution went on the wane (no pun intended). And that's a shame. Yes, it's true that you don't need an opener when there are no cans (as is the case with an MRE). Still, even the Army says that these little beauties are a lot more than just can openers (see attached news release from the Fort Monmouth Public Affairs Office).

So we invite you to offer a salute to our little friend, the NSN 7330-00-242-3506.

38 ways to use the P-38
(From a Fort Monmouth Public Affairs Office news release)
By Master Sergeant Steve Wilson

1. can opener
2. seam ripper
3. screwdriver
4. clean fingernails
5. cut fishing line
6. open paint cans
7. window scraper
8. scrape around floor corners
9. digging
10. clean out groove on Tupperwear lids
11. reach in and clean out small crack
12. scrape around edge of boots
13. bottle opener
14. (in the field) gut fish
15. (in the field) scale fish
16. test for "doneness" when baking by camp fire
17. prying tool
18. strip wire
19. scrape pane in the field
20. lift key on flip top cans
21. chisel
22. barter
23. marking tool
24. deflating tires
25. clean sole of boot/shoe
26. pick teeth
27. measurement
28. striking flint
29. stirring coffee
30. puncturing plastic coating
31. knocking on doors
32. Morse Code
33. box cutter
34. opening letters
35. write emergency messages
36. scratch an itch
37. save as a souvenir
38. rip off rank for on-the-spot promotion

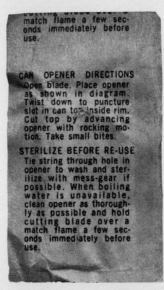

In its original packaging, the NSN 7330-00-242-3506 is becoming a collector's item. This one came out of a Vietnam-era case of C-rats.

SAVORY GREEN BEANS
KOREAN WAR

This recipe pairs tomatoes and green beans but adds a bit of a kick with the spices. The cloves and sugar give this dish a distinctive flavor. It isn't necessarily a holiday dish, but the green and red colors can make it work.

FOR AN ARMY OF 100

RATIONS: 25 pounds green beans*
Salt
Boiling water
2 pounds chopped onions
1 cup melted bacon fat
$^1/_2$ ounce ground cloves
6 tablespoons sugar
3 tablespoons salt
Pepper to taste
1 No. 10 can tomatoes
   –or– 2 14-ounce cans catsup

FOR AN ARMY OF 10

RATIONS: 2 $^1/_2$ pounds green beans
Salt
Boiling water
$^3/_4$ cup onions
1 $^1/_2$ tablespoons bacon fat
1 tablespoon cloves
1 $^3/_4$ teaspoons sugar
$^3/_4$ teaspoon salt
Pepper to taste
1 $^1/_3$ cups tomatoes
   –or– 5 $^2/_3$ tablespoons catsup

ORDERS: Wash beans and remove ends. Cut into pieces or leave whole. Add to boiling salted water. Heat to boiling point; reduce heat and simmer about 30 minutes or until tender. Drain. Fry onions in bacon fat. Combine cloves, sugar, cooked onions, salt, pepper, and tomatoes. Heat to boiling point. Combine beans and tomato mixture just before serving.

*Three No. 10 cans green beans may be substituted for fresh green beans.

SLANG

Critter fritters
(Navy; contemporary): Fried meat-like items served in crew's mess. See "mystery meat."

SPICED FRUIT CUP
OPERATION IRAQI FREEDOM

This one is a quick fruit dish that combines that can of fruit in the pantry with easily obtainable fresh fruit. The military chef could use this recipe for any meal—breakfast, lunch, or supper—as it makes a nice addition to the menu at any time of the day.

FOR AN ARMY OF 100

RATIONS: 1 gallon plus 2 quarts fruit cocktail, including liquids
$\frac{1}{8}$ teaspoon ground cinnamon
$\frac{1}{3}$ teaspoon ground nutmeg
1 $\frac{5}{8}$ cups brown sugar
3 quarts plus 2 $\frac{1}{2}$ cups fresh apples, unpeeled and diced
3 quarts plus 1 $\frac{3}{8}$ cups fresh orange sections, peeled and diced

FOR AN ARMY OF 10

RATIONS: 2 $\frac{1}{4}$ cups fruit cocktail, including liquids
Dash cinnamon
Dash nutmeg
$\frac{1}{2}$ cup brown sugar
4 cups fresh apples, unpeeled and diced
3 $\frac{1}{2}$ cups orange sections, peeled and diced

ORDERS: Drain fruit cocktail and reserve juice. Combine juice with ground cinnamon, ground nutmeg, and brown sugar. Combine fruit cocktail, apples, and oranges. Pour chilled syrup over fruits; mix lightly. Cover and chill until serving.

Don't call them "jarheads," and don't call them late for chow. A few good men go through the chow line during field exercises in 2003.

SUGARED PARSNIPS
WORLD WAR II

Parsnips have a sweet, nutty taste. They have a long shelf life if stored properly, making them an excellent addition to the kitchen pantry. As a starchy component to a balanced meal, parsnips are more nutritious than the more popular potato.

FOR AN ARMY OF 100

RATIONS: 30 pounds parsnips
2 quarts beef stock
2 pounds sugar
1 ounce ground
cinnamon
Salt and pepper to taste

FOR AN ARMY OF 10

RATIONS: 3 pounds parsnips
$^3/_4$ cup beef stock
$^1/_3$ cup sugar
2 tablespoons cinnamon
Salt and pepper to taste

ORDERS: Scrape and wash the parsnips thoroughly, slice lengthwise, and place them into a well-greased bake pan. Season to taste with salt and pepper. Pour the beef stock over them. Cover the bake pan to prevent evaporation. Bake in a slow oven (200°–250°—18 to 20 counts*) for about an hour, or until tender. Sift the sugar and cinnamon together. About 5 minutes before taking the dish out of the oven sprinkle this cinnamon-sugar mixture over the parsnips and replace in the oven until the top begins to brown.

*See page 150.

HE HAD HIS HEART SET ON PÂTÉ DE FOIE GRAS!

NAVY CHOW IS THE BEST!
TAKE ALL YOU CAN EAT
EAT ALL YOU TAKE!

DON'T BE FINICKY.

The Navy served up hot, nutritious chow, and sailors were expected to eat it—all of it—and like it. Posters, such as one from World War II, appeared in mess halls to remind the sailors of their duty.

VEGETABLE STEW
KOREAN WAR

This dish is almost a meal in itself. Lots of vegetables and a savory gravy. Add a little garlic for flavor, if desired. The base cook could easily prepare this dish from items on the shelf—using canned vegetables if fresh were not available.

FOR AN ARMY OF 100

RATIONS: 3 $3/4$ pounds cooked, diced carrots

3 $3/4$ pounds cooked, diced potatoes

3 pounds cooked, diced celery

1 No. 10 can wax beans

1 No. 10 can peas

1 $1/2$ cups sifted flour

6 tablespoons sugar

3 tablespoons salt

1 teaspoon pepper

1 No. 10 can tomatoes

1 $1/2$ cups butter or bacon fat

FOR AN ARMY OF 10

RATIONS: 1 $1/4$ cups cooked, diced carrots

1 $1/4$ cups cooked, diced potatoes

1 cup cooked, diced celery

1 cup wax beans

1 cup peas

7 tablespoons sifted flour

1 $3/4$ teaspoons sugar

$3/4$ teaspoon salt

Pepper to taste

1 cup tomatoes

7 tablespoons butter or bacon fat

ORDERS: Drain cooked carrots, potatoes, and celery. Mix beans and peas; heat. Drain. Combine flour, sugar, salt, pepper, and tomatoes; mix well. Heat. Combine all vegetables; add butter or bacon fat. Heat thoroughly.

Noodles Jefferson
Buttered Hominy
Corn Fritters
Corn Pilaf
Deviled Eggs
Macaroni Republic
Zesty Rotini Pasta Salad
Oatmeal Fritters
Scalloped Noodles
Spanish Rice
Tossed Green Rice

CHAPTER 5
SIDE DISHES

NOODLES JEFFERSON
KOREAN WAR

Thomas Jefferson was a philosopher, scientist, farmer, inventor, architect, diplomat, musician, dreamer, politician, and noodle maven. The man had a knack of spreading himself around.

It was during his stint as ambassador to France, just after the American Revolution, that Jefferson first encountered pasta. This dish was nothing new in Italy, of course, and had been a staple for centuries. But it had recently been "discovered" by the elite of French society, and it was all the rage in Paris during the 1780s.

Jefferson acquired a pasta-making machine while on a trip to Italy in 1787. Following that tour, he took the machine, along with a large quantity of pasta, home to Virginia. Unfortunately, leaky wooden ships being what they were, his consignment didn't make it back in the best of shape. The machine was broken and the pasta was unrecognizable.

So upon his return, Jefferson took time out of his busy schedule of founding a country, being secretary of state, building (and rebuilding) Monticello, and all that, to sit down and design his own macaroni machine. (His original drawing is in the Library of Congress.)

History does not record whether our third president preferred his macaroni with cheese, or his spaghetti with marinara sauce. But we know for a fact that Mr. Jefferson did some noodling around at Monticello, and that's good enough for us.

This recipe was named in Jefferson's honor by the Army and has appeared in mess halls since the Korean War.

FOR AN ARMY OF 100

RATIONS: 6 gallons warm water
3 tablespoons salt
3 tablespoons salad oil
9 pounds egg noodles
2 $\frac{1}{2}$ cups butter, melted
1 tablespoon black pepper
2 pounds grated Parmesan cheese

FOR AN ARMY OF 10

RATIONS: 4 cups warm water
$\frac{1}{2}$ teaspoon salt
$\frac{1}{2}$ teaspoon salad oil
4 $\frac{1}{2}$ cups egg noodles
$\frac{1}{4}$ cups butter or margarine, melted
Pepper to taste
1 $\frac{1}{4}$ cup grated Parmesan cheese

ORDERS: Add salt and oil to water, heat to a rolling boil. Slowly add noodles, stirring constantly, until water boils again. Cook about 8 to 10 minutes, or until tender. Drain thoroughly. Add butter and pepper to noodles. Stir well. Add cheese. Toss well.

BUTTERED HOMINY
VIETNAM WAR

Hominy, according to those formal cookbooks, is hulled corn with the germ removed. According to us, it is the kernel without the hard outer covering or that little nub at the tip. It is the interior "meat" of the kernel.

Traditional recipes from the Southland would have you grind dry hominy to produce grits, and serve it as a side dish at breakfast. Hominy is actually pretty versatile, and it can be served boiled, fried, or baked.

American colonists would boil raw hominy in a weak lye solution to loosen the hulls and prepare the grain for cooking. That may be a bit much for today. On the other hand, there is something to be said for "fresh"; hominy does lose something when it goes through the canning process. A dash of Tabasco sauce will add some needed kick.

FOR AN ARMY OF 100
RATIONS: 8 $\frac{3}{4}$ quarts
canned hominy
2 teaspoons
black pepper
3 tablespoons salt
1 cup butter
or margarine
$\frac{1}{2}$ cup fresh
chopped parsley –or–
2 tablespoons paprika

FOR AN ARMY OF 10
RATIONS: 3 $\frac{1}{2}$ cups
canned hominy
Dash pepper
$\frac{3}{4}$ teaspoon salt
1 $\frac{1}{2}$ tablespoons
butter or margarine
2 $\frac{1}{4}$ teaspoons
chopped fresh
parsley –or–
$\frac{1}{2}$ teaspoon paprika

ORDERS: Add pepper and salt to hominy. In a saucepan on the stovetop, heat slowly, without draining, for 20 minutes. Drain. Add butter or margarine. Garnish with parsley or paprika.

Good powder is no more a munition of war than good food.
—Edward S. Farrow, U.S. Army, in *Mountain Scouting, a Hand-book for Officers and Soldiers on the Frontier*, 1881

SLANG

Mystery meat
Unidentified meatlike substance served in an Army mess hall

CORN FRITTERS
WORLD WAR II

The people who are in charge of such things have designated July 16 as "National Corn Fritters Day." If it were up to us, we'd have stopped at February 4, "National Stuffed Mushroom Cap Day." Also known as corn oysters, corn fritters have earned their own special day just by being the sweet fried dumplings that they are. They're a good side dish and are served as one would biscuits or bread. Sifting the dry ingredients ensures an even distribution of the baking powder and salt (the leavenings in the recipe).

FOR AN ARMY OF 100

RATIONS: 2 No. 10 cans cream-
style corn
24 eggs
2 $^1/_2$ ounces salt
10 pounds flour
5 ounces baking
powder
2 gallons milk or water

FOR AN ARMY OF 10

RATIONS: 2 $^1/_2$ cups cream-
style corn
3 eggs
1 $^1/_2$ teaspoons salt
2 cups flour
2 $^3/_4$ teaspoons
baking powder
3 cups milk or water

ORDERS: Beat the corn and eggs together thoroughly. Sift together the salt, flour, and baking powder three times. Add a portion of the liquid, then a portion of the sifted dry ingredients, stirring well. Continue until dry ingredients are thoroughly mixed in, regulating the quantity of liquid to make a thick batter that just drops off the spoon. A thin batter makes a poor product. Using a large basting spoon, drop spoonfuls into hot fat and fry until brown. The hot fat should be just deep enough to cover the fritters. Serve hot with syrup.

CORN PILAF
KOREAN WAR

The corn and pimiento in this recipe can brighten up a rice side dish for any kind of meat. Browning the rice before cooking gives it a slightly nutty flavor and adds to the aroma of the dish. It can be made vegetarian style by substituting vegetable oil for the fat.

FOR AN ARMY OF 100

RATIONS: 2 pounds rice, uncooked
1 pound fat
3 $\frac{1}{2}$ quarts water
2 $\frac{1}{2}$ tablespoons salt
$\frac{3}{4}$ quart onions, chopped
3 No. 10 cans corn
1 $\frac{1}{2}$ cups pimiento

FOR AN ARMY OF 10

RATIONS: $\frac{1}{3}$ cup rice, uncooked
3 tablespoons fat
$\frac{2}{3}$ cup water
$\frac{2}{3}$ teaspoon salt
$\frac{1}{2}$ cup onions, chopped
2 cups canned corn
$\frac{1}{2}$ cup pimiento

ORDERS: Wash rice thoroughly; drain to remove excess water. Cook the rice in half the fat until brown, stirring occasionally. Combine rice, water, salt, and onions. Heat to boiling point; reduce heat and simmer 30 minutes or until rice is tender. Add corn, pimientos and remaining fat; mix well. Heat to serving temperature.

"When it's smokin', it's cookin'; when it's burnin', it's done." That's our motto.
—A front-line mess sergeant, depicted by Norman Mailer in his 1948 Pulitzer Prize–winning novel, *The Naked and the Dead*

DEVILED EGGS
KOREAN WAR

What, exactly, is the "devil" in deviled eggs? Tempted as we are to say that it is the cholesterol content (Get it? Tempted . . . devil?), we shall refrain. The term "deviled" gained usage in Europe during the eighteenth century when it was used to describe a highly spiced food. This deviled egg recipe is not highly spiced, but is a traditional rendering of this American favorite.

FOR AN ARMY OF 100

RATIONS: 100 hard-cooked eggs
$^1/_2$ 14 $^1/_2$ -ounce can
   evaporated milk
$^1/_2$ pint hot water
   (for milk)
3 cups mayonnaise
2 tablespoons salt
2 tablespoons dry
   mustard
1 cup vinegar

FOR AN ARMY OF 10

RATIONS: 10 hard-cooked eggs
$^2/_3$ cup evaporated milk
1 $^1/_2$ tablespoons
   hot water (for milk)
$^1/_4$ cup mayonnaise
$^1/_2$ teaspoon salt
$^1/_2$ teaspoon
   dry mustard
1 $^1/_2$ tablespoons
   vinegar

ORDERS: Remove shells from eggs; cut in half lengthwise. Remove yolks from eggs; mash yolks thoroughly. Combine mashed yolks and remaining ingredients; mix thoroughly. Refill whites with yolk mixture, using approximately 1 tablespoon filling for each half egg white. Top each half egg with a dash of paprika.

NOTE: Ten ounces (1 ounce for 10) of finely chopped celery or 4 ounces (2 1/2 teaspoons for 10) finely chopped pimientos may be added to the yolk mixture.

"I'm always glad when we get fish. Then I'm sure it's not horsemeat!"

MACARONI REPUBLIC
KOREAN WAR

We will admit that Americans didn't invent pasta. We will even, albeit grudgingly, admit that macaroni was imported. But it is going to take a whole lot of convincing to get us to back down from our assertion that macaroni and cheese isn't somehow locked into place with Mom and apple pie. This could be called the "Yankee Doodle" recipe. Macaroni has been part of American diets from American Revolution times. Colonists boiled macaroni for an hour or more (it was a little different then from the box of elbows we can find on the supermarket shelves). This is a wonderful casserole that is reminiscent of home-baked macaroni and cheese dishes many of us had as children. It can be the main dish for a meal or a side dish with ham or chicken.

FOR AN ARMY OF 100

RATIONS: 8 pounds macaroni
12 tablespoons salt
12 gallons boiling water
6 14 $1/2$ -ounce cans evaporated milk
$3/4$ gallon water (for milk)
1 quart butter
7 7-ounce cans pimiento, finely chopped
1 cup parsley, chopped
2 $1/2$ pounds bread, diced
12 tablespoons salt
1 tablespoon celery salt
1 tablespoon dry mustard
5 pounds cheese, shredded
60 eggs, beaten
Paprika

FOR AN ARMY OF 10

RATIONS: 3 cups macaroni
3 $1/2$ tablespoons salt
8 cups boiling water
1 $1/4$ cups evaporated milk
1 $1/4$ cups water (for milk)
$1/3$ cup butter
$2/3$ cup pimiento, finely chopped
1 $1/2$ tablespoons parsley, chopped
1 cup bread, diced
3 $1/2$ teaspoons salt
$1/4$ teaspoon celery salt
$1/4$ teaspoon dry mustard
1 $2/3$ cups cheese, shredded
6 eggs, beaten
Paprika

ORDERS: Add macaroni slowly to boiling water; boil 10 to 15 minutes or until tender. Drain well. Mix milk and water; heat. Add butter, pimientos, parsley, bread crumbs, salt, pepper, celery salt, mustard, and cheese. Reheat and simmer until cheese is melted. Add milk and crumb mixture to beaten egg. Mix macaroni and crumb mixture. Place into well-greased baking pans. Sprinkle with paprika. Bake in a slow oven (325°) until firm. Garnish with parsley and serve hot.

MACHINE-GUNNED EGGS

When a man hasn't had fresh eggs in a long time, he'll go through anything to get them. This was the case with the Eighth Regiment of the First Cavalry Division, while they were cleaning the Japanese out of this area.

After long months of jungle fighting, the regiment finally got an issue of fresh eggs, and the chow line began forming several hours before breakfast. Then, just as the serving started, a Japanese machine gun starting peppering the area. Everyone ducked— on the stove. The only sounds heard above the enemy woodpecker and our own M1 fire were cries of "Don't let the eggs burn!"

One at a time, as their numbers came up, the cavalrymen left their cover, dashed up to the stove, hastily fried from two to four eggs and dashed off to safety to eat them.

Eventually someone got around to knocking out the enemy.

From *Yank* magazine, 1944

"SEE IF YOU CAN BRING SOME
KETCHUP NEXT TRIP!"

ZESTY ROTINI PASTA SALAD
OPERATION IRAQI FREEDOM

This salad makes a nice picnic or barbecue dish. Since it should be made well ahead of serving, it is great for a party or cold buffet supper.

FOR AN ARMY OF 100

RATIONS: 2 gallons, 2 quarts water
1 tablespoon salt
1 tablespoon olive oil
1 gallon, $3/4$ quarts rotini noodles
1 quart plus 2 cups low-fat Italian salad dressing
1 $1/2$ cups grated Parmesan cheese
$1/2$ cup sesame seeds
3 tablespoons poppy seeds
$1/4$ cup plus $1/3$ table-spoon paprika
2 quarts plus $3/4$ cup fresh tomatoes, chopped
3 quarts plus 1 $3/8$ cups fresh cucumbers, chopped
1 quart plus 2 $1/8$ cups fresh green peppers, chopped
1 quart plus $1/4$ cup fresh onions, chopped

FOR AN ARMY OF 10

RATIONS: 4 cups water
$1/4$ teaspoon salt
$1/4$ teaspoon olive oil
1 $1/2$ cups rotini noodles
$1/2$ cup low-fat Italian salad dressing
$1/3$ cup grated Parmesan cheese
2 tablespoons sesame seeds
$3/4$ tablespoon poppy seeds
1 teaspoon paprika
1 cup fresh tomatoes, chopped
2 cups fresh cucumbers, chopped
1 cup fresh green peppers, chopped
$3/4$ cup fresh onions, chopped

ORDERS: Add salt and salad oil to water; heat to a rolling boil. Add rotini slowly, stirring constantly until water boils again. Cook about 10 to 12 minutes or until rotini is tender; stir occasionally. DO NOT OVERCOOK. Drain. Rinse with cold water. Combine dressing with cheese, sesame seeds, poppy seeds, and paprika. Add to rotini. Toss lightly. Add tomatoes, cucumbers, peppers, and onions. Toss lightly. Cover and refrigerate at least 3 hours or until flavors are blended. Keep refrigerated until ready to serve.

SLANG

DFAC (pronounced dee-fak): Dining facility. Call it a "mess hall" or a "chow hall" and you'll be marked as an old-timer (and not necessarily with a great deal of respect).

OATMEAL FRITTERS
WORLD WAR I

This recipe, from the turn of the twentieth century, has rather exacting instructions. And the cook reading this recipe from the rarefied atmosphere of the twenty-first century kitchen might wonder why the baking powder is added only bit by bit to small portions of the batter. There's a good reason.

In 1916, when the *Manual for Army Cooks* was published, leavening agents were not as stable as they are today. It was customary at this time for baking powder, in particular, to be added as one of last ingredients in a recipe to ensure proper rising. When preparing these fritters in the home kitchen with contemporary ingredients, it is not necessary to take this precaution. Still you might want to follow these instructions to the letter to get the full military experience.

FOR AN ARMY OF 60
RATIONS: 1 gallon oatmeal
mush
1 pound sugar
8 ounces baking
powder

FOR AN ARMY OF 6
RATIONS: 1 $\frac{1}{2}$ cups
oatmeal mush
3 tablespoons sugar
1 $\frac{1}{2}$ teaspoon
baking powder

ORDERS: First you need to make the oatmeal mush (see recipe, page 78). Mix the mush, sugar, and sufficient flour to make a stiff batter. To one-eighth of the mixture add 1 ounce (1/3 teaspoon) of baking powder and mix thoroughly, then with a tablespoon cut pieces about half the size of an egg; drop into deep smoking fat and fry until a golden brown. After frying remove them from the fat with a skimmer; put in a colander to drain, after which place into a bake pan to keep warm. Repeat each eighth of the mixture in the same manner. Dust the fritters with powdered sugar and arrange in tiers on plates. To improve them, add six eggs and a few drops of extract to each gallon of mush.

I saw some Marines eating a plate of nails. The sissies were the ones who had to put salt on them.
—Bob Hope, in *Don't Shoot, It's Only Me*

SCALLOPED NOODLES
VIETNAM WAR

This casserole can also be made with ground beef or ham substituted for the bacon. If using ground beef, brown it first, draining well, and alternate the beef with the noodles, tomatoes, onions, and cheese.

FOR AN ARMY OF 100

RATIONS: 3 No. 10 cans
tomatoes
(2 $\frac{1}{4}$ gallons)
1 $\frac{1}{2}$ tablespoons
black pepper
6 tablespoons salt
3 gallons noodles
4 gallons boiling water
6 tablespoons salt
4 $\frac{1}{2}$ quarts cheddar
cheese, shredded
2 pounds bacon, cut
into 1-inch pieces
4 tablespoons paprika

FOR AN ARMY OF 10

RATIONS: 3 cups canned
tomatoes
$\frac{1}{4}$ teaspoon pepper
1 $\frac{3}{4}$ teaspoons salt
4 $\frac{1}{2}$ cups noodles
6 cups boiling water
1 $\frac{3}{4}$ teaspoons salt
1 $\frac{3}{4}$ cups cheddar
cheese, shredded
$\frac{1}{3}$ cup bacon, cut
into 1-inch pieces
1 teaspoon paprika

ORDERS: Combine tomatoes, salt, and pepper. Heat to boiling point; reduce heat and simmer 30 minutes. Add noodles slowly to salted boiling water; boil 15 to 20 minutes or until tender. Drain. Arrange alternate layers of noodles, tomatoes, and cheese in a well-greased pan. Sprinkle bacon on top of noodle mixture. Sprinkle with paprika. Bake in a 350° oven for 25 to 30 minutes or until bacon is crisp.

Cocoa powder is neither.

—Lessons learned by a helicopter crewman

THE GRUNT'S HIERARCHY OF CHOW

Hot garrison chow is better than hot C-rations, which in turn is better than cold C-rations, which is better than no food at all. All of these, however, are preferable to cold rice balls (given to you by guards) even if they do have the little pieces of fish in them.

SPANISH RICE
KOREAN WAR

In military cookbooks from the time of the Plains Indians Wars through World War II, the word "Spanish" in the title of a recipe seems to mean tomatoes are involved. This is a tasty and filling dish. Add some ground beef or turkey to make a casserole dinner for the family.

FOR AN ARMY OF 100

RATIONS: 2 No. 10 cans tomatoes
3 gallons water
3 pounds onions, chopped
2 pounds green peppers, chopped
1 cup salt
1 tablespoon pepper
12 pounds rice, uncooked
9 pounds cheese, shredded

FOR AN ARMY OF 10

RATIONS: $^2/_3$ cup tomatoes
4 $^1/_2$ cups water
$^1/_4$ cup onions, chopped
$^3/_4$ cup green pepper, chopped
1 $^1/_2$ tablespoons salt
$^1/_4$ teaspoon pepper
2 $^1/_2$ cups rice, uncooked
3 $^1/_3$ cups cheese, shredded

ORDERS: Combine tomatoes, water, onions, peppers, salt, and pepper; heat to the boiling point. Wash rice; drain thoroughly. Add rice to tomato mixture. Cover and heat to boiling point. Reduce heat and simmer until rice is tender, stirring frequently. Remove from heat; add cheese. Stir until cheese is melted.

SLANG

Bean rag
The pennant flown aboard ships of the U.S. Navy to denote the crew was at mess.

"MEAL REFUSING TO EXIT"

When the American military phased out C-rations in the early 1980s, they were replaced amid much fanfare with the new Meals Ready to Eat (MREs, in accepted military shorthand). The fanfare and excitement pretty much died out as soon as troops started to eat them. The standing joke was that there were at least three lies contained in the name.

During the Gulf War, there was widespread belief that MREs were a leading, if not *the* leading, cause of constipation among U.S. elements of the Coalition Forces. Hence, this little piece of slang. One other popular theory held that the abbreviation stood for Meals Rejected by Everybody, but this one seems to be going away. A lot of work has been done on MREs since Operation Desert Storm. They're manufactured to rather exacting specifications and must maintain their quality for at least three years if stored at 80 degrees Fahrenheit, and six months if stored at one hundred degrees. The packaging must be durable enough to survive being thrown out of an airplane. (Thrown out on purpose, as in an airdrop.)

The menus have been updated, too. A number of entrees have been discontinued (including the dreaded Chicken a la King) and new ones added. There are now three vegetarian meals. Gone, but living in infamy, is the powdered drink mix. It was dropped in 1993 after managing to hang in there for about fifty years, from World War II through the Korean War, the Vietnam War, and the Gulf War (and in all that time, no one ever really knew what it was). From that time forward, soldiers have had to find other things with which to scrub their field ovens.

(Related to this, also from the Gulf War, is "ree," which is even shorterhand for MRE.)

TOSSED GREEN RICE
VIETNAM WAR

Finding green rice in the fridge, particularly back in those heady days of first apartments, was not necessarily a good thing. But in this recipe, even Mom would approve of the color.

The sautéed onions, peppers, and parsley give the rice a wonderful flavor and its green color. Other vegetables, such as zucchini, summer squash, peas, or carrots, can be added to make this a main-dish meal in itself. Add a bit of Tabasco or cayenne pepper for a little kick.

FOR AN ARMY OF 100

RATIONS: 10 pounds rice, parboiled
3 gallons cold water
6 tablespoons salt
$1/2$ cup salad oil
3 cups green onions, thinly sliced
2 pounds sweet peppers, minced
1 cup shortening
$4 1/4$ cups parsley, minced
2 teaspoons black pepper
2 tablespoons monosodium glutamate

FOR AN ARMY OF 10

RATIONS: $1 1/2$ cups rice
3 cups water
$1 3/4$ teaspoons salt
$2 1/4$ teaspoons salad oil
$1/4$ cup green onions, thinly sliced
$1/3$ cup sweet peppers, minced
$1 1/2$ tablespoons shortening or oil
$1/3$ cup parsley, minced
$1/4$ teaspoon black pepper
Dash monosodium glutamate (if desired)

ORDERS: Combine rice, water, salt, and salad oil; bring to a boil. Stir occasionally. Cover tightly and simmer 13 minutes. DO NOT STIR. If rice is not tender, continue to cook 2 to 3 minutes longer. Sauté onions and pepper in hot shortening until lightly browned. Add sautéed vegetables, parsley, pepper, and monosodium glutamate (MSG) to rice. Fold carefully until well blended. Steam dry 7 to 10 minutes and toss.

Before heading off on patrol into the Vietnam jungle, troops made sure they were supplied with a good quantity of C-4 explosive compound. With the consistency of modeling clay, this plastic explosive was potent when strategically placed near something that needed blowing up (trees in landing zones, for example; or tunnels where the VC would lurk).

Completely inert unless triggered by a blasting cap, it was both safe and easy to carry. It could take a bullet without going off. It was also flammable, which had the happy effect of helping to start a fire in a tropical rain forest. Just pinch off a little nub and roll it into a ball, put your Zippo to it, and you could get a nice little flame going. Just the thing to heat the morning coffee or warm a can of Charlie rations.

There were several problems with this, however—the first of which was that C-4 is extremely poisonous. If even a little residue was stuck to knives or fingers, it could be injested, and there were cases of C-4 poisoning reported at base hospitals.

The second problem showed up when trying to put out the fire. If you stomped on it, the combination of heat and compression was enough to set off an explosion.

But the biggest problem was that whatever was used to heat coffee was no longer available to blow stuff up with. And there were times when stuff really, really needed to be blown up. And it was at times like these that men wondered just how much that morning coffee was worth.

CHAPTER 6
BREADS

ARMY FIELD BREAD
SPANISH-AMERICAN WAR

This bread requires a little bit of thought and preparation, because the first thing you need to do is get yourself a shovel and dig yourself a hole out in the back yard. This is field bread and would have been baked while the troops were on maneuvers, camping in the field.

If you don't feel like having another hole in your back yard, the next best thing is to make a mud oven. This is a structure, above ground, with a hole in the side where you can slip in your pan. A frying pan and open flame will work, too.

It doesn't get much more authentic than this.

RATIONS: 5 quarts flour
1 $^2/_3$ tablespoons yeast
  powder
Salt
1 tablespoon lard
  or drippings
Water

ORDERS: Take 5 quarts of flour and 1 2/3 tablespoons of yeast powder; mix thoroughly while dry, adding a little salt to suit the taste; then mix in well 1 tablespoonful of dripping or lard; then add water, in small quantities at a time, until a biscuit dough is made; knead lightly.

Dig a hole in the ground 18 or 20 inches in diameter and depth, and burn a fire in it 5 to 6 hours. Take a government mess pan and cut off about 1 1/2 inches of the rim, leaving a rough edge. Into this pan put dough enough to fill it two-thirds full; cover with another mess pan. Then take out all the cinders from the fire except a bed two or three inches deep; upon this place the mess pans and surround and cover with hot cinders. Spread with a covering of earth and leave for 5 or 6 hours. The bread will not burn, as in rising it will not reach the bottom of the upper mess pan. The rough-cut edges of the lower mess pan afford egress to any gases that may be discharged.

Field Bread Baked in a Frying Pan

ORDERS: Prepare the dough as described to the left. Grease the frying pan and set it over hot embers until the grease begins to melt; put the dough, rolled to a thickness of 1/2 inch, in the pan and set on the fire; shake the pan every few minutes to prevent the dough from sticking.

DUMPLINGS
VIETNAM WAR

Dumplings are essentially biscuits that are boiled or steamed rather than baked. Cooked on top of a stew, they absorb some of the flavor of the mixture beneath them and are a delicious addition to a meal. Try them with Slum (Slumgullion, page 87). It may be a little anachronistic, but boy is it good.

Just make sure you give the dumplings plenty of time to steam all the way through, or they will be doughy.

FOR AN ARMY OF 100

RATIONS: 2 $\frac{1}{2}$ quarts flour, sifted

6 $\frac{3}{4}$ tablespoons baking powder

1 $\frac{1}{8}$ cups nonfat dry milk

2 $\frac{1}{4}$ tablespoons salt

6 eggs

5 $\frac{1}{2}$ cups water

FOR AN ARMY OF 10

RATIONS: 1 cup flour, sifted

2 teaspoons baking powder

2 tablespoons nonfat dry milk

$\frac{1}{2}$ teaspoon salt

1 egg

$\frac{2}{3}$ cup water

ORDERS: Mix and sift dry ingredients together. Add eggs and water to flour mixture; mix well. Drop by No. 16 scoop or 1/4 cup on top of simmering stew. Cover kettle. Do not open kettle during cooking time. Cook 15 minutes.

APPLE ROLLS
KOREAN WAR

One of the best-smelling kitchens you'll ever encounter is where Apple Rolls are baking. It just don't get no better than this. Like apple pie, there's something about baked apples that's comforting and patriotic and delicious all at the same time.

Made with canned applesauce, this recipe could be served with breakfast or as a light dessert.

FOR AN ARMY OF 100

RATIONS: 6 $\frac{1}{2}$ quarts flour, sifted
7 $\frac{1}{2}$ tablespoons baking powder
3 tablespoons salt
3 pounds shortening
2 $\frac{1}{2}$ No. 1 cans evaporated milk
1 $\frac{1}{4}$ quarts water (for milk)
1 $\frac{1}{2}$ quarts applesauce
1 quart shortening, melted
1 $\frac{1}{2}$ quarts brown sugar

FOR AN ARMY OF 10

RATIONS: 3 cups flour
2 teaspoons baking powder
$\frac{3}{4}$ teaspoon salt
$\frac{1}{2}$ cup shortening
$\frac{1}{4}$ cup evaporated milk
$\frac{1}{2}$ cup water (for milk)
$\frac{2}{3}$ cup applesauce
$\frac{1}{3}$ cup shortening
$\frac{2}{3}$ cup brown sugar

ORDERS: Sift together the flour, baking powder, and salt; cut in the shortening. Add milk that has been combined with water to flour mixture; mix to soft dough. Roll to approximately 1/2-inch thickness. Spread with applesauce and roll as for jelly roll. Cut in 1-inch slices. Melt fat, add sugar, spread in bottom of baking pan. Place rolls fairly close together, cut side down, on top of sugar mixture. Bake at 400° for 20–25 minutes. Remove from pans and serve warm.

BAKING POWDER BISCUITS
KOREAN WAR

For most of us, the smell of fresh biscuits or baking bread is one of life's little treasures. Of course, the allure may have been lost a bit on the baker who was up to his elbows in dough several times a day. But there was compensation in knowing that the K.P.s would be coming to clean up after him.

Here's a hint: If you don't have a biscuit cutter in your kitchen, the rim of a drinking glass is usually the right size to give round, flaky biscuits. Just make sure to dip it in flour as you use it, to prevent sticking.

Here's another hint: Get your K.P.s lined up before the flour starts to fly.

This recipe, in its Army-sized proportions, would turn out 25 pounds of biscuit dough or 212 biscuits.

FOR AN ARMY OF 100

RATIONS: 12 quarts flour
12 ounces baking powder
6 tablespoons salt
1 $\frac{3}{4}$ quarts shortening
2 14-$\frac{1}{2}$ ounce cans evaporated milk
4 quarts water (for milk)

FOR AN ARMY OF 10

RATIONS: 4 $\frac{3}{4}$ cups flour
4 tablespoons baking powder
1 $\frac{3}{4}$ teaspoons salt
11 tablespoons shortening
1/2 cup evaporated milk
1 $\frac{1}{2}$ cups water

ORDERS: Sift flour, baking powder, and salt together; add shortening; blend until mixture resembles coarse crumbs. Do not mix to a paste. Mix milk and water; add to dry ingredients, mixing only enough to combine dry and liquid ingredients. Additional mixing will cause biscuits to be tough. Roll 1/2-inch thick; cut dough into biscuits with floured biscuit cutter.

Dough may be cut into 2- or 2 1/2-inch squares to eliminate the second handling of leftover pieces as when a round cutter is used. Place in baking pans. Bake in hot oven (450°) about 15 minutes.

NOTE: Biscuits may be brushed with melted shortening or milk before baking to make an even brown on top.

BRAN MUFFINS
KOREAN WAR

Military cooks knew the mess had to keep the troops moving, and they accepted and fulfilled that mission in every way possible. Perhaps, sometimes, they moved faster than others.

Bran is a good dietary fiber, and bran muffins are a delicious way of getting that fiber into our diets.

FOR AN ARMY OF 100

RATIONS: 5 14 $\frac{1}{2}$ -ounce cans evaporated milk
3 quarts water (for milk)
6 quarts bran
1 quart granulated sugar
$\frac{3}{4}$ quart shortening
24 eggs, beaten
6 quarts flour, sifted
1 $\frac{1}{3}$ cups baking powder
8 tablespoons salt

FOR AN ARMY OF 10

RATIONS: 1 cup evaporated milk
1 $\frac{1}{4}$ cups water
2 $\frac{1}{2}$ cups bran
$\frac{1}{3}$ cup granulated sugar
5 $\frac{2}{3}$ tablespoons shortening
3 eggs, beaten
2 $\frac{1}{2}$ cups flour
2 $\frac{1}{4}$ tablespoons baking powder
2 $\frac{1}{4}$ teaspoons salt

ORDERS: Mix milk and water. Add bran; soak about 10 minutes. Mix sugar and shortening; stir until smooth. Add beaten egg; mix well. Add soaked bran; mix well. Sift flour, baking powder, and salt together; add to bran mixture, stirring only until dry and liquid ingredients are combined. Spread in greased muffin pans. Bake in hot oven (425°) about 20 minutes.

HARDTACK
CIVIL WAR

In the East, this was called hard bread. The Navy called it ship's biscuit. Federal forces during the Civil War gave it the moniker "hardtack." It was a staple in military diets for nearly a hundred years (hardtack finally went away after the Spanish-American War).

You might almost think of them as salted crackers. But the original was thicker and larger (about 3 inches square). And they were dense. And they were hard.

Soldiers, when they were being kind, called them "tooth dullers" and "sheet iron." But hardtack was filling. If you had time, you could break it down and add some water or milk, perhaps throw in some fruit or meat and make a stewy kind of thing they called "sloosh."

RATIONS: 4 cups flour
4 teaspoons salt
Water

ORDERS: Mix flour and salt thoroughly. Add water to form a dough that is elastic, but not sticky. Roll to about 1/2 inch in thickness. Bake in a 400° oven until slightly brown. Remove from oven and let cool. Prick with a fork or nail over surface of bread. Score with a knife into rectangles. Place in a 200° oven for about two hours or until hard. Yields about 44 crackers.

Civil War knife, fork, plate, and hardtack

HOE CAKES
REVOLUTIONARY WAR

This was reputedly George Washington's favorite breakfast. He'd smother them with sorghum, molasses, and butter.

It was a quick meal, often made while on the march, a simple and easy concoction. If you weren't too fussy, or were in a hurry, you'd put the dough on a heated rock. If you were feeling particularly genteel, you'd put it in a pan suspended over the fire. Sometimes you'd just throw the dough right into the fire (this changed it from hoe cake to ash cake). During the Civil War, the troops would put the dough on the end of their bayonets and hold it over the open flames of the campfire. Some recipes called for yeast and an overnight rising.

FOR A SMALL GROUP AROUND THE CAMPFIRE

RATIONS: 1 cup cornmeal
$\frac{1}{2}$ teaspoon salt
1 tablespoon lard
Boiling water

ORDERS: Mix cornmeal and salt. Add lard and enough boiling water to make a well-formed dough. Shape into small, thin loaves. Prepare hoe (griddle) with hot lard or other grease; spoon on batter. Hold over fire until one side is done. Flip hoe cake and cook on other side.

NOTE: Can be baked in well-greased pan at 375° for about 25 minutes

A relic of the American Revolution, this shovel was beaten into a skillet for use over the campfires by American forces camped at Jockey Hollow, New Jersey.

SAUSAGE CORN BREAD
VIETNAM WAR

During the Civil War, the troops did a good bit of foraging to supplement their issued rations. There also were sutlers in the larger camps, who would sell the soldiers a variety of items—both household and foodstuffs. There's a story concerning the troops of Confederate general John B. Hood, who in 1862 had a brush with a sutler just outside Richmond. The man was offering fresh sausage from his wagon, and Hood's Texans took full advantage, buying the lot and frying it up. All was fine until one soldier discovered a claw . . . then another man found a claw. It seems the main ingredient was not pork, but cat.

Rather than include that Civil War recipe, we thought it better to provide one from the Vietnam War era.

If you prepare fresh pork sausage in this dish, be sure to drain it well. Whether served as a breakfast dish or as a side dish, this is a tasty way to prepare corn bread.

FOR AN ARMY OF 100

RATIONS: 4 $\frac{1}{2}$ quarts flour, sifted
3 $\frac{1}{3}$ quarts corn meal
3 cups granulated sugar
3 tablespoons salt
10 tablespoons baking powder
2 $\frac{2}{3}$ cups nonfat dry milk
3 $\frac{1}{4}$ quarts warm water
22 eggs, beaten
1 quart shortening, melted
8 21-ounce cans pork sausage links, drained

FOR AN ARMY OF 10

RATIONS: 2 $\frac{1}{4}$ cups flour, sifted
1 $\frac{1}{2}$ cups corn meal
$\frac{1}{4}$ cup sugar
$\frac{3}{4}$ teaspoon salt
1 tablespoon baking powder
5 $\frac{2}{3}$ tablespoons nonfat dry milk
1 $\frac{1}{2}$ cups warm water
2 eggs, beaten
$\frac{1}{3}$ cup shortening, melted
1 pound sausage links, precooked

ORDERS: Blend dry ingredients thoroughly. Reconstitute milk; add eggs and shortening. Add to dry ingredients. Mix only until dry ingredients are moistened. Pour into well-greased pan. Rinse sausage thoroughly with hot water. Drain. Arrange sausages crosswise on top of batter. Bake 30 minutes at 350° or until done.

NOTE: Serve for breakfast with eggs or baked beans.

HOT ROLLS
VIETNAM WAR

During the early days of the Civil War, the city of Washington, D.C., became an armed camp, with troops billeted just about everywhere. The unfinished Capitol building did its duty. Horses were stabled on its grounds. Troops slept in the halls. And the basement was converted into a great bakery. Bread has been known as the "staff of life," and indeed it was one of the most important and sought-after rations for the hungry soldier. The American military has always tried to provide bread in some form with the daily food ration. These hot rolls, from the Vietnam War era, are some of the best—military or civilian—we've ever tried.

FOR AN ARMY OF 100

RATIONS: $2/_3$ cup active dry yeast
3 $1/_2$ cups warm water (105°–110°)
2 $3/_4$ quarts cold water
3 $1/_3$ cups granulated sugar
5 tablespoons salt
10 $2/_3$ quarts flour
1 $3/_4$ cups nonfat dry milk
3 $3/_4$ cups shortening

FOR AN ARMY OF 10

RATIONS: 1 tablespoon dry active yeast
5 $2/_3$ tablespoons warm water (105°–110°)
1 $1/_4$ cups cold water
7 tablespoons sugar
2 teaspoons salt
4 $1/_3$ cups flour
8 $1/_4$ teaspoons nonfat dry milk
5 tablespoons shortening

ORDERS: Sprinkle yeast on top of water. Mix well. Let stand 5 minutes; stir. DO NOT USE TEMPERATURES OVER 110°. Dissolve sugar and salt in water in mixer bowl. Add yeast solution. Combine flour and dry milk; add to liquid mixture. Use dough hook to mix 1 minute or until flour is incorporated into liquid. Add shortening and continue mixing at medium speed 10 minutes or until dough is smooth and elastic. Dough temperature should range between 78° to 82°. Ferment: Set dough in warm place (80°) for 1 1/2 hours or until double in bulk. Punch: Divide dough into three pieces; round up and let rest for 10 to 20 minutes. Roll each piece into a long rope of uniform diameter. Cut rope into pieces about 1 inch thick, weighing 1 1/2 to 2 ounces. Make up as desired. Place rolls on greased pans and brush with butter wash. Proof at 90° until double in size. Bake 15–20 minutes or until golden brown. Brush with butter wash immediately after baking.

QUICK COFFEE CAKE
VIETNAM WAR

There's nothing like a piece of good coffee cake and a hot cup of joe in the morning. This recipe has the right blend of eggs, flour, and cinnamon to make it perfect for a quick grab-and-go breakfast.

FOR AN ARMY OF 100

RATIONS: 3 pounds, 8 ounces
sifted flour
6 $3/4$ tablespoons
baking powder
1 $1/2$ cups nonfat
dry milk
1 $1/2$ tablespoons salt
2 quarts sugar
15 eggs, beaten
3 $3/4$ cups melted
shortening
2 tablespoons vanilla
6 $1/2$ cups water
TOPPING:
1 $1/2$ quarts sifted flour
1 tablespoon ground
cinnamon
$1/4$ teaspoon salt
2 cups brown sugar
1 $1/2$ cups melted
butter or margarine
ICING:
$1/4$ cup butter or
margarine
1 $3/4$ quarts powdered
sugar
1 teaspoon vanilla
$3/4$ cup boiling water

FOR AN ARMY OF 10

RATIONS: 1 $1/2$ cups sifted flour
1 $1/2$ teaspoons baking
powder
1 $1/2$ tablespoons
nonfat dry milk
$1/2$ teaspoon salt
$3/4$ cup sugar
2 eggs, beaten
$1/3$ cup melted
shortening
$1/2$ teaspoon vanilla
$2/3$ cup water
TOPPING:
$2/3$ cup flour
$1/4$ teaspoon cinnamon
Dash salt
4 tablespoons brown
sugar
7 teaspoons melted
butter or margarine
ICING:
1 tablespoon butter or
margarine
$2/3$ cup powdered sugar
$1/4$ teaspoon vanilla
3 $1/2$ teaspoons
boiling water

ORDERS: Mix and sift dry ingredients together. Add shortening, vanilla, and water to eggs. Add dry ingredients to egg mixture and mix lightly. Pour batter evenly into greased pans. Combine topping ingredients; mix to a coarse crumb. Sprinkle evenly over batter in each pan. Bake about 30 minutes at 375° or until done. Combine icing ingredients; mix until smooth. Spread over cooled cake in each pan.

TEMPERATURE GAUGE, HAND-TYPE

The Army really does think of everything. It really does have the best interests of the troops at heart.

Ever on the lookout for ways to do right by the troops, the Army began recruiting and training bakers during the First World War. Standard issue were special field ovens so the bread would be fresh (this was pretty much the final nail in the coffin for hard-tack, by the way; but no one seemed to mind).

As our armed forces grew in size and sophistication, so did their equipment. Well, most of their equipment. The field ovens

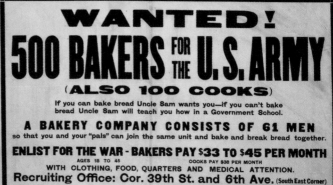

pretty much stayed the same right through World War II. But that was jake; they worked fine: You put the raw food in, and it usually came out either cooked or heading in that general direction. There wasn't much more that you could ask of an oven.

Oh... there was this one thing. If it wasn't too much trouble. A thermometer would be nice. Standard, GI-issue field ovens didn't have them. During World War II, the Army's keen sense of precision moved it to develop a method that would allow the cook to determine just how hot the oven was and how long the biscuits would need to bake.

To the surprise of almost no one, pain was involved.

The "Count" method was developed and published in the Army's Technical Manual TM-10-405: *The Army Cook*, printed in 1942. Now, the way we understand it, the cook would fire up the oven, wait a little bit, and then stick his hand in. He would then proceed to count, slowly please, the number of seconds he was able to keep his hand in the oven (before, presumably, he began to scream). The lower the count, the hotter the oven (unless he was a real wimp). If the poor guy could stand it for eighteen to twenty counts, the oven was a mild 200°–250°, and he would have to wait a little longer before trying it again. If he could only take it for eight to ten seconds, then the oven was what the Army termed "hot." (Honestly. You just can't make this stuff up.)

Here are the Army's instructions for using the Count method for determining temperature.

Counts	Degrees Fahrenheit	Common Names for Oven Temperatures
8	450 to 500	Hot
9 to 12	400 to 450	Quick
12 to 16	325 to 450	Medium
16 to 18	250 to 325	Moderate
18 to 20	200 to 250	Slow

Apparently, the screaming was loud enough to result in thermometers being added to field ovens following the Korean War. By that time, any cooks left over from World War II had their hash marks.

Tartar Sauce
Barbecue Sauce
Mock Maple Sirup
Raisin Sauce
Spanish Sauce
Spiced Tomato Gravy
Tomato Catsup

CHAPTER 7
SAUCES & GRAVIES

TARTAR SAUCE
VARIOUS CONFLICTS

Believe it or not, the tartar sauce we most commonly enjoy today with fish and other seafood began as a savory sauce for steak tartare. Historians have yet to discover the first person to dip a piece of fish into this mayonnaise-based sauce, but GIs surely relished this condiment for a fish fry.

Here are three recipes for tartar sauce that demonstrate the changes in military supply and the soldiers' tastes. Note the addition of spices, eggs, and fresh herbs to the recipe as time goes by.

FISH SAUCE

From the Mexican War era:

RATIONS: 2 cups boiling water
2 tablespoons butter (melted)
2 tablespoons flour
Pepper and salt to taste
Vinegar to taste

ORDERS: Mix butter and flour into a smooth paste in a saucepan over a fire. Pour in boiling water, stirring constantly. Add a little vinegar for an acid taste.

CREAM SAUCE FOR CODFISH

From the World War I era:

FOR AN ARMY OF 60

RATIONS: 1 pound fat, butter preferred
4 cans evaporated milk
$1/_2$ pound onions, minced
$1/_2$ pound pickles, minced
6 hard-boiled eggs, minced, if desired

FOR AN ARMY OF 6

RATIONS: $1/_3$ cup fat, butter preferred
$2/_3$ cup evaporated milk
$1 1/_2$ tablespoons onions, minced
$1 1/_2$ tablespoons pickles, minced
1 hard-boiled egg, minced, if desired

ORDERS: Thicken 1 gallon (1 1/2 cups) of boiling water with a flour batter and season well with salt and pepper; let come to a boil and add the fat, milk, onions, and pickles; whip well and spread over fish. The sauce may be improved by the addition of 6 hard-boiled eggs (1 egg), chopped fine.

TARTAR SAUCE

From the Korean War era:

FOR AN ARMY OF 100

RATIONS: 1 gallon mayonnaise
10 hard-boiled eggs
1 pound finely
chopped dill pickles
1 pound finely
chopped onion –or–
12 tablespoons
dehydrated onion
4 ounces (4 bunches)
finely chopped
parsley
$1/_4$ pound prepared
mustard
$1/_2$ pint vinegar

FOR AN ARMY OF 10

RATIONS: 1 $1/_2$ cups mayonnaise
1 hard-boiled egg
1 $1/_2$ tablespoons
finely chopped dill
pickle
$1/_3$ cup finely
chopped onion –or–
3 $1/_2$ teaspoons
dehydrated onion
2 $1/_4$ teaspoons finely
chopped parsley
2 $1/_4$ teaspoons pre-
pared mustard
1 $1/_2$ teaspoon
vinegar

ORDERS: Mix ingredients together thoroughly. If dehydrated
onions are used, cover with cold water, soak
1 hour, drain, and add to other ingredients.
Mix thoroughly.

An eighteenth-century
camp broiler, also called
a brazier. The square
base held coals, and
containers were placed
on the hinged grill
for cooking.

BARBECUE SAUCE
WORLD WAR II

Many barbecue sauces are closely guarded secrets, passed down from generation to generation. President Lyndon Baines Johnson would've told you there really was only one kind of barbecue, and it could be found only in Texas. LBJ loved his BBQ, and would regularly invite foreign heads of state to his ranch for a bash. (Some sources will tell you he did it because some of those heads looked a little silly holding paper plates, with a bit of cole slaw on their ties.)

While not wishing to offend the memory of LBJ or his native Lone Star State, we must point out that they know their 'Q in Kansas City. And the Carolinas take a back seat to no one.

The vinegar helps this recipe lean a little toward the Carolinas. You may want to use it as a start, and then add your own secrets.

FOR AN ARMY OF 100

RATIONS:
1 gallon catsup
1 gallon vinegar
2 to 3 cups dry mustard
2 tablespoons red pepper
3 tablespoons black pepper
$3/4$ cup chili powder
2 medium-size cloves of garlic
$1/2$ cup salt

FOR AN ARMY OF 10

RATIONS:
1 $1/2$ cups catsup
1 $1/2$ cups vinegar
3 tablespoons to $1/4$ cup dry mustard
$1/2$ teaspoon red pepper
3 $1/4$ teaspoons black pepper
3 $1/2$ teaspoons chili powder
Garlic to taste
2 $1/4$ teaspoons salt

ORDERS: Combine ingredients and bring to a boil. Let boil 2 hours or until it begins to thicken. Mix well and keep it stirred.

Why does man kill? He kills for food. And not only food: frequently there must be a beverage.

—Woody Allen

CHOW—FOOD

The precise origin of the term "chow" has been lost (but that's not a problem for us; we'd rather have a good story than one that's been dulled by easily verified facts).

There are a number of theories about the word. Perhaps the most plausible traces it to the seventeenth century, when England began to rule the waves, and the East India Company's ships were visiting ports throughout Africa and Asia. Business was booming. There was, of course, a little problem with communication. Between Europe, Africa, India, Southeast Asia, the islands of the Pacific, and mainland China, more than a few languages were in play (there were more than a few just in China).

A hybrid language of commerce was developing. It was a mixture of European tongues (primarily Portuguese and English), Indian dialect, and a variety of Asian terms—all spoken with a Chinese accent. It was called Pidgin (a term that itself was a corrupted version of the Chinese for "do business").

Anyway, our theory states that chow is actually a slang term, derived from Pidgin. The Pidgin word for a cargo of food (derived from an Indian dialect and spoken with a Chinese accent, remember) is chow. Over the past 400 years or so, the term has changed from the cargo to the thing itself. Sailors picked up the term first. No doubt, once the ships started carrying troops, the term became a staple of military jargon.

Variations include:
Chow down—to eat a really big meal
Chowhound—one who likes to eat a big meal
Chowda—a kind of soup made with clams that they eat in New England (OK, we just made that one up)

MOCK MAPLE SIRUP
KOREAN WAR

There is nothing in the world quite as American as a maple tree in late winter with a bucket attached. Warming days, cool nights, and you know what's coming.

Real maple syrup is a joy. Unfortunately, the military isn't always in a position to stop for joy. So in a pinch, with a stack of hotcakes on the counter, the military cook made this "mock" maple sirup from stores on hand. (And that isn't an error: the real stuff is spelled with a *y*; the mock stuff uses an *i*.)

This isn't from Vermont, but it's not bad.

FOR AN ARMY OF 100

RATIONS: 6 pounds brown sugar
2 ½ quarts boiling water
3 tablets vanilla or 1 tablespoon vanilla extract

FOR AN ARMY OF 10

RATIONS: 1 ½ cups brown sugar
¾ cup boiling water
¼ teaspoon vanilla extract

ORDERS: Add sugar to boiling water; stir until sugar is dissolved. Heat to boiling point; boil 10 minutes or until a thin "sirup" is formed, without stirring. Remove from heat. Cool, add vanilla extract.

Thanksgiving dinner never tasted so good to this GI in Korea in 1950. Dinner, with all the trimmings, was delivered fresh and hot to troops who had just been in combat.

RAISIN SAUCE
KOREAN WAR

A note on this Korean War–era recipe suggests serving this sauce over baked ham or tongue. It does make a wonderful glaze for a baked ham. But we confess that glazing a tongue, even in the interest of historical research, was a little too much to ask.

So, while we recommend it for ham, when it comes to tongue . . . you're on your own.

FOR AN ARMY OF 100

RATIONS: 1 pound raisins
Hot water to cover raisins
3 quarts cider or pineapple juice
3 quarts water
3 tablespoons salt
1 tablespoon pepper
2 $\frac{1}{2}$ cups brown sugar
12 tablespoons cornstarch
Cold water for cornstarch
1 $\frac{1}{2}$ cups butter
Juice from 3 lemons
–or– $\frac{2}{3}$ cup vinegar

FOR AN ARMY OF 10

RATIONS: $\frac{2}{3}$ cup raisins
Hot water to cover raisins
1 $\frac{1}{4}$ cups cider or pineapple juice
1 $\frac{1}{4}$ cups water
$\frac{3}{4}$ teaspoon salt
$\frac{1}{4}$ teaspoon pepper
$\frac{1}{4}$ cup brown sugar
3 $\frac{1}{2}$ teaspoons cornstarch
Cold water for cornstarch
7 teaspoons butter or margarine
Juice from $\frac{1}{2}$ lemon
–or– 1 tablespoon vinegar

ORDERS: Wash raisins. Cover with hot water; soak until plump. Drain. Mix cider or pineapple juice and water; add raisins, salt, pepper, and brown sugar; heat. Mix cornstarch and a little cold water; add to raisin mixture. Heat to boiling point; boil 5 minutes or until thick, stirring constantly. Add butter and lemon juice or vinegar; mix well.

SPANISH SAUCE
WORLD WAR II

During World War II, cooks following *The Army Cook* technical manual were told to use this sauce on fish. During World War I, cooks following their manual had been told to use this recipe on meat. It's the same recipe. Perhaps this means that military cookery continued to evolve between the wars. Or, perhaps, it doesn't mean that at all. Perhaps it means nothing. We just thought we'd point it out.

FOR AN ARMY OF 100

RATIONS: 2 pounds fat
4 pounds minced onions
2 No. 10 cans tomatoes
5 cloves garlic
5 ounces red pepper, ground
2 gallons beef stock
Salt to taste
Flour to thicken

FOR AN ARMY OF 10

RATIONS: $1/3$ cup fat
$3/4$ cup onions, minced
$2 1/2$ cups tomatoes
1 clove garlic
$2/3$ cup red pepper
3 cups beef stock
Salt to taste
Flour to thicken

ORDERS: Fry onions and garlic in shallow fat until well done, then place in a double boiler with the tomatoes, beef stock, and seasoning and heat thoroughly. Thicken slightly with a flour batter.

Cases of K-rations are delivered to the front lines in France shortly after D-Day during World War II.

SPICED TOMATO GRAVY
KOREAN WAR

Soldiers from all over the United States would have been familiar with tomato gravy as a sauce for rice or potatoes. Seasonings varied by regional tastes as cooks added spices familiar to diners. This recipe, from the 1950 Army technical manual, cautions the cook on the use of seasonings in this spicy gravy.

FOR AN ARMY OF 100

RATIONS: 2 pounds fat from
cooked meat
2 pounds flour
$\frac{1}{2}$ clove garlic
1 $\frac{1}{2}$ gallons hot
stock
2 No. 2 $\frac{1}{2}$ cans
tomatoes
Nutmeg, mace, ground
cinnamon, and
ground cloves
to taste

FOR AN ARMY OF 10

RATIONS: $\frac{1}{3}$ cup fat from
cooked meat
$\frac{2}{3}$ cup flour
Garlic to taste
2 $\frac{1}{2}$ cups hot stock
$\frac{3}{4}$ cup canned
tomatoes
Nutmeg, mace, ground
cinnamon, and
ground cloves
to taste

ORDERS: Pour clear fat from roasting or frying pan
after meat is cooked, allowing brown particles to
remain. Measure fat. Return measured fat to pan;
add crushed garlic and fry until brown. Add flour;
stir until smooth. Continue cooking over low heat
until flour is brown. Add hot stock gradually, stirring constantly. (If no stock is available, hot water
may be used.) Add strained crushed tomatoes.
Stir. Heat to boiling point, boil 2 minutes or until
thick, stirring constantly. Add salt, pepper, and
other spices to taste.

WHAT'S A C-RATION?

Officially, the Army called it a "Meal, Combat, Individual." Beginning in World War II and continuing into the 1980s, it was a package issued to soldiers in the field by the U.S. Quartermaster Corps.

The first-generation C-ration was developed in 1938 and weighed five pounds, ten ounces. Plans called for ten distinct varieties of canned meat combinations, such as beef stew, beef with noodles, family-style dinner, lamb stew, and Irish stew.

Field trials were undertaken in 1940, and the consensus of the participants was that the cans were too large and bulky, the meat lacked variety, and there were just too many beans. The official Army report called it "one of the best field rations ever issued." Figures. With the first significant issue of C-rations in 1941, the cans were reduced from sixteen ounces to twelve ounces. The main dishes consisted of meat and beans, meat-and-vegetable stew, and, for variety, meat-and-vegetable hash. In addition to the canned entree, the package contained a "B2" unit consisting of cheese, crackers, candy, a canned dessert, and an accessory pack with salt and pepper, a beverage powder—usually coffee—chewing gum, a plastic spoon, a "John Wayne" (can opener), and a pack of four cigarettes.*

With modifications, this basic configuration was used for the better part of the next forty years, until phased out and replaced with MREs (Meals Ready to Eat).

* Cigarettes were eliminated from the basic C-ration package in 1975, in deference to health concerns.

A full case of C-rations is displayed during their introduction at the start of World War II.

TOMATO CATSUP
CIVIL WAR

Next time you're on vacation and driving through the Great Midwest, you might want to take a quick side trip to Collinsville, Illinois. It would certainly be worth your while because there, just off Route 159, is one of the largest bottles of catsup you may ever see (it's probably the biggest you will ever need to see, anyway). Placed on the National Register of Historic Places in 1995, this 170-foot-high water tower was built in 1949 to resemble a bottle of catsup. Now, the tower isn't right on Route 159, so you may have to stop and ask directions. But don't worry; they know where it is in Collinsville.

Catsup, of course, was around long before 1949. The term has been in use as far back as the late seventeenth century. This recipe is from the nineteenth century and was used during the American Civil War. Hardtack and catsup? Perhaps. Maybe you can ask when you get to Collinsville.

RATIONS: 4 quarts tomatoes
1 pint vinegar
3 tablespoons salt
2 tablespoons dry mustard
2 tablespoons black pepper
3 dried red peppers, broken
$\frac{1}{2}$ ounce allspice or mace

ORDERS: Cook until smooth.

Thanksgiving 1861 with the Federal armies. Two years before Abraham Lincoln officially proclaimed the national holiday, Alfred Rudolph Waud sketched this camp scene.

CHAPTER 8
DESSERTS

BANANA CREAM PIE
KOREAN WAR

In 1951, the military undertook a massive survey of the troops regarding food and mess preferences. The most up-to-date and scientific sampling methods were employed. The questions were pretested to eliminate bias.

When the results were tabulated and cross-checked, it turned out that Banana Cream Pie was the favorite recipe of all served in mess halls around the world. This is the winning recipe.

By the way, the least favorite was Rice Pudding. That recipe is presented elsewhere in this chapter, just in case you'd like to do your own survey.

FOR AN ARMY OF 100

RATIONS: 8 14 $\frac{1}{2}$ -ounce cans
evaporated milk
4 quarts water
(for milk)
1 quart cornstarch
2 $\frac{1}{2}$ quarts granulated sugar
3 tablespoons salt
1 $\frac{1}{4}$ cups butter
36 eggs, slightly
beaten
4 tablespoons vanilla
15 pounds bananas

FOR AN ARMY OF 10

RATIONS: 1 $\frac{1}{2}$ cups evaporated
milk
1 $\frac{1}{2}$ cups water
(for milk)
$\frac{1}{3}$ cup cornstarch
$\frac{3}{4}$ cup granulated
sugar
$\frac{3}{4}$ teaspoon salt
2 tablespoons butter
4 eggs, slightly
beaten
1 teaspoon vanilla
1 $\frac{1}{2}$ pounds bananas

ORDERS: Mix milk and water. Mix cornstarch and half the sugar. Add 1 1/2 quarts (2/3 cup) milk mixture; stir until smooth. Add beaten eggs and mix thoroughly. Mix salt, remaining sugar, and remaining milk mixture together; heat to boiling point. Pour about a fourth of the boiling liquid over the egg and starch mixture. Stir until well mixed. Add egg mixture to boiling milk mixture, stir constantly, and bring to a boil. Add butter and vanilla. Mix well; let cool until lukewarm. Pour half the cooked filling into baked pie shells. Cover with a layer of sliced bananas. Pour remaining filling over banan-as. Cover with meringue if desired.

SLANG

Pogey
(World War II): Candy and sweets. Primarily (and still) a Marine Corps term.

APPLE BROWNIES
VIETNAM WAR

Some things stand by themselves and need no further explana-
tion. Apples. Brownies. What else do you need to know?

FOR AN ARMY OF 100

RATIONS: 2 quarts dehydrated
apples
3 $\frac{1}{2}$ quarts water
2 $\frac{1}{4}$ quarts flour,
sifted
2 tablespoons salt
2 $\frac{1}{4}$ tablespoons
baking powder
1 $\frac{1}{2}$ tablespoons
baking soda
4 $\frac{1}{2}$ cups shortening
2 $\frac{1}{4}$ quarts
granulated sugar
11 eggs, slightly
beaten
2 tablespoons
cinnamon
4 tablespoons vanilla
1 quart chopped nuts
1 $\frac{1}{2}$ cups raisins,
washed and drained

FOR AN ARMY OF 10

RATIONS: $\frac{3}{4}$ cup dehydrated
apples
1 $\frac{3}{4}$ cups water
1 cup sifted flour
$\frac{1}{2}$ teaspoon salt
$\frac{2}{3}$ teaspoon baking
powder
$\frac{1}{3}$ teaspoon baking
soda
$\frac{1}{3}$ cup shortening
$\frac{3}{4}$ cup granulated
sugar
1 egg, slightly beaten
$\frac{1}{2}$ teaspoon
cinnamon
1 teaspoon vanilla
$\frac{1}{3}$ cup chopped nuts
$\frac{1}{4}$ cup raisins,
washed and drained

ORDERS: Combine apples and water. Bring to a boil and
simmer 15 minutes or until tender. Let apples cool
in juice, drain, and chop. Set aside. Sift together
dry ingredients. Using beater at medium speed,
cream shortening and sugar 4 minutes or until
light. Add eggs, cinnamon, and vanilla to creamed
mixture. Beat until light. Fold flour mixture into
creamed mixture. Carefully fold apples, nuts, and
raisins into mixture. Do not overmix. Mixture will
be thick. Spread in a greased pan. Bake about 40
minutes in a 350° oven. Cool and cut into squares.

NOTE: One No. 10 can drained applesauce (1 1/4 cups) can
be substituted for dehydrated apples and water.

APPLE PIE FILLING
WORLD WAR II

Even the Army didn't think the boys would go to war without apple pie. It never made it into a C-ration, but it was a mainstay at camp mess halls. It can be made with either canned or fresh apples—depending on the location of the mess and if the supplies had arrived.

FOR AN ARMY OF 100

RATIONS: 3 No. 10 cans apples
1 quart water
2 cups cornstarch
1 pint water
(for cornstarch)
2 $\frac{1}{4}$ quarts granulated
sugar
$\frac{1}{2}$ tablespoon salt
$\frac{1}{2}$ cup butter
1 tablespoon cinnamon
Juice of 3 lemons

FOR AN ARMY OF 10

RATIONS: 3 $\frac{3}{4}$ cups canned
apples
$\frac{1}{3}$ cup water
9 $\frac{1}{2}$ teaspoons cornstarch
9 $\frac{1}{2}$ teaspoons water
(for cornstarch)
$\frac{3}{4}$ cup granulated sugar
Dash of salt
7 teaspoons butter
$\frac{1}{4}$ teaspoon cinnamon
Juice of $\frac{1}{2}$ lemon

ORDERS: Drain juice from apples. Add water to juice; heat to boiling point. Add sugar and salt; stir until sugar is dissolved. Remove from heat. Mix cornstarch and water; stir until smooth. Add slowly to hot juice. Heat to boiling point; boil 2 minutes or until thick, stirring constantly. Add butter, cinnamon, lemon juice, and apples; mix well. Cool before placing in unbaked pie shells.

These GIs hadn't even gotten off the boat from their crossing when they were introduced to British hospitality. Hot tea and cake were handed up by members of the Women's Voluntary Service early in World War II.

ARTILLERY PIE
CIVIL WAR

You just don't see too many good uses for suet in the kitchen anymore. Particularly when you're talking about desserts.

Suet is what they call the trimmings off a good piece of beef. The fat. It wasn't all that long ago (well, OK, yes, it was) when it was considered a delicacy and found its way into all sorts of things. Like desserts. Like Artillery Pie.

FOR A PLATOON OF 22
RATIONS: 8 pounds bread
1 pound suet
4 dozen apples
2 pounds sugar

FOR A PLATOON OF 10
RATIONS: 4 pounds bread
$\frac{1}{2}$ pound suet
2 dozen apples
$\frac{1}{2}$ pound sugar

ORDERS: Melt the suet in a frying pan; cut the bread into slices 1/4 inch in thickness; dip each piece into the melted fat and place in the oven to dry. Peel apples; boil them; mash with the sugar. Cover bottom of the baking dish with the bread, cover bread with some apples, then more bread over that, then apples, and so on until all is used. Bake for 20 minutes. This may be made with any kind of fruit.

It was no uncommon sight to see a brigade or division, which but a moment before was marching in solid column along the road, scattered over an immense field searching for luscious blackberries. And it was wonderful to see how promptly and cheerfully all returned to the ranks when the field was gleaned.

—Carlton McCarthy, *Detailed Minutiae of Soldier Life in the Army of Northern Virginia*

BAKED INDIAN PUDDING
WORLD WAR II

Corn meal, the main ingredient in this dessert, was known as Indian meal to the early American settlers. By adapting traditional British boiled pudding to foodstuffs available in the New World, early American cooks created this sweet pudding. The Army updated the recipe a bit by adding additional spices.

FOR AN ARMY OF 100

RATIONS: 4 pounds corn meal
2 pounds flour
1 quart molasses
4 14 $\frac{1}{2}$ -ounce cans evaporated milk, diluted with 4 pints water
$\frac{1}{2}$ pound butter
2 gallons boiling water
$\frac{1}{2}$ ounce cinnamon
1 ounce ginger

FOR AN ARMY OF 10

RATIONS: $\frac{3}{4}$ cup corn meal
$\frac{1}{3}$ cup flour
$\frac{1}{3}$ cup molasses
$\frac{3}{4}$ cup evaporated milk, diluted with $\frac{3}{4}$ cup water
1 $\frac{1}{2}$ tablespoons butter
3 cups boiling water
1 tablespoon cinnamon
2 tablespoons ginger

ORDERS: Mix molasses and corn meal together and pour boiling water over it. Add butter, salt, and spices. When mixture is cool, pour milk over, but do not stir into the pudding. Bake in a slow oven (200°– 250°, 16–18 counts) from 2 to 3 hours. Take care that it does not burn. Serve hot.

World War II–era linen-finish comic postcard. This was the sort of thing sent home from the camps.

BROWN BETTY
WORLD WAR II

This dessert has been a familiar part of the American table since colonial times. A "Betty" is any pudding made with bread crumbs and fruit. The flour batter mentioned in this recipe is simply a couple of tablespoons of flour mixed thoroughly with cold water.

FOR AN ARMY OF 100
RATIONS: 15 pounds bread or
      bread scraps
      10 pounds sugar,
      caramelized
      4 pounds currants or
      other dried tart fruit
      5 gallons water
      Flour batter to thicken

FOR AN ARMY OF 10
RATIONS: 3 cups bread or bread
      scraps
      2 cups sugar,
      caramelized
      $3/_4$ cup currants or
      other dried tart fruit
      7 $1/_2$ cups water
      Flour batter to thicken

ORDERS: Dice bread into 1-inch cubes and brown in a slow oven. Add the caramelized sugar and the fruit to the water; thicken slightly with a flour batter and pour over the diced bread. Bake in a medium oven (325°–400°, 12–16 counts) about 20 minutes and serve with sauce.

RICE PUDDING
PLAINS WAR

This is a traditional recipe and was considered a real treat. The sweet milk made it a standout.

RATIONS: 1 quart of clean rice   1 pound sugar
      6 quarts sweet milk   2 teaspoons salt
      (or the equivalent   Enough grated
      of condensed milk)   nutmeg and ground
                               cinnamon to flavor

ORDERS: Cover rice with a portion of the milk and let soak for 2 hours; then add remainder of the milk and sift into this the sugar, salt, and spices. Place into a well-greased dishpan and bake 2 1/2 hours in a slow (225°) oven. Serve hot or cold.

CHOCOLATE SPONGE
KOREAN WAR

A sponge pudding creates two layers as it chills—a spongy bottom layer and a quivery gelatin layer on top.

This recipe requires a little bit of work to get it right (just separating 84 yolks from 84 whites requires a little bit of work), but the results are certainly worth the effort. Serve it with a dollop of whipped cream.

FOR AN ARMY OF 100

RATIONS: 1 $^3/_4$ quarts cold water
1 $^1/_2$ cups plain gelatin
1 $^3/_4$ quarts warm water
2 $^1/_3$ quarts granulated sugar
1 tablespoon salt
1 pound cocoa
84 egg yolks, slightly beaten
84 egg whites, stiffly beaten
6 tablespoons vanilla

FOR AN ARMY OF 10

RATIONS: $^3/_4$ cup cold water
7 teaspoons plain gelatin
$^3/_4$ cup hot water
1 cup granulated sugar
$^1/_4$ teaspoon salt
$^1/_2$ cup cocoa
9 egg yolks, slightly beaten
9 egg whites, stiffly beaten
1 $^3/_4$ teaspoons vanilla

ORDERS: Pour cold water over gelatin; mix and allow to stand 5 minutes. Mix hot water, sugar, salt, and cocoa together. Heat to boiling point; boil about 3 minutes or until smooth. Add gelatin; stir until thoroughly dissolved. Add slightly beaten egg yolks. When mixture begins to thicken, add stiffly beaten egg whites and vanilla. Chill. Serve with whipped cream or whipped evaporated milk.

The original rain forest café? Front-line grunts pass through the chow line during the Vietnam War.

EGGLESS CAKE
KOREAN WAR

Some recipes disappear because they're just not all that popular. But some disappear because they are no longer needed. This one falls into the latter category.

Preparing a sweet dessert from field rations was no easy task in the days before refrigeration or advanced supply techniques. The cooks cobbled together what they could from what was available, and made a cake such as this for the soldiers.

This recipe uses stewed fruit as part of the liquid ingredients. It produces a dense, dark cake, one rather on the sweet side.

The recipe disappeared from military cookery after World War II. Advances in food management and technology allowed the cook access to eggs (fresh, frozen, or dehydrated), and the reason why Eggless Cake was required in the first place simply went away.

FOR AN ARMY OF 100

RATIONS: 10 $\frac{1}{4}$ pounds flour
5 $\frac{1}{4}$ ounces baking powder
3 $\frac{1}{2}$ ounces cinnamon
2 ounces flavoring extract
15 pounds sugar
2 $\frac{1}{4}$ pounds fat (butter, lard, or lard substitute)
4 pounds dried fruit, stewed and ground
10 quarts milk or 10 cans evaporated milk
10 pints water (for milk)

FOR AN ARMY OF 10

RATIONS: 4 cups flour
3 $\frac{3}{4}$ teaspoons baking powder
3 $\frac{1}{4}$ teaspoons cinnamon
1 teaspoon flavoring extract
1 cup sugar
$\frac{1}{2}$ cup fat (butter, lard, or lard substitute)
$\frac{3}{4}$ cup dried fruit, stewed and ground
3 $\frac{3}{4}$ cups milk

ORDERS: Cream the fat, sugar, and flavoring extract. Sift together the flour, baking powder, and cinnamon three times and add this and the fruit to the creamed mixture with the milk. Water may be used in place of milk but does not make as good a cake. Stir well and bake about 40 minutes in a moderate oven (250°–325°, 16–18 counts). Serve plain or iced.

FRUIT BARS
KOREAN WAR

America's eating habits have changed through the years. Prior to World War II, for example, the midday meal was the largest of the day, with the evening repast typically being much lighter.

Cookies were a favorite dessert item for the evening meal on base. These fruit bars made for a nice light touch of sweetness after a meal.

These are also good lunch-box cookies and keep well in an airtight container.

FOR AN ARMY OF 100

RATIONS: 1 $1/4$ quarts granulated sugar

2 $1/2$ tablespoons salt

5 tablespoons cinnamon

2 $1/2$ tablespoons ginger

2 $1/2$ tablespoons baking soda

$7/8$ quart shortening

16 eggs

1 quart molasses or brown sugar

2 $1/2$ quarts seedless raisins or other fruit

5 quarts flour, sifted

FOR AN ARMY OF 10

RATIONS: $1/2$ cup granulated sugar

$2/3$ teaspoon salt

1 $1/2$ teaspoons cinnamon

$2/3$ teaspoon ginger

$2/3$ teaspoon baking soda

$1/3$ cup shortening

2 eggs

$1/3$ cup molasses or brown sugar

1 cup seedless raisins or other fruit

2 cups flour, sifted

ORDERS: Combine sugar, salt, cinnamon, ginger, soda, and shortening; stir until light and fluffy. Mix eggs and molasses or brown sugar; beat well. Add egg and molasses mixture to sugar mixture in three parts, beating until light after each addition. Add fruit and flour; mix until a smooth dough is formed. Scale dough into 14-ounce pieces. Roll each piece into a roll about 1 inch in diameter and 24 inches long. Place four rolls in pan and flatten. Bake at 350° to 400° for 18 to 20 minutes.

MOLASSES CRUMB COOKIES
KOREAN WAR

Bar cookies were a favorite choice of the mess cook. Once baked, they could easily be cut into squares and put on serving plates for the chow line. This recipe is full of spices and has the distinctive taste of molasses.

FOR AN ARMY OF 100

RATIONS: 4 quarts flour, sifted
3 tablespoons baking powder
2 tablespoons baking soda
2 tablespoons salt
2 tablespoons ginger
2 tablespoons cinnamon
2 tablespoons ground cloves
1 $\frac{1}{2}$ quarts cake crumbs
$\frac{3}{4}$ quart shortening
1 $\frac{1}{2}$ quarts granulated sugar
10 eggs, beaten
$\frac{7}{8}$ quart molasses
1 $\frac{1}{4}$ cups water

FOR AN ARMY OF 10

RATIONS: 1 $\frac{1}{2}$ cups flour, sifted
$\frac{3}{4}$ teaspoon baking powder
$\frac{1}{2}$ teaspoon baking soda
$\frac{1}{2}$ teaspoon salt
$\frac{1}{2}$ teaspoon ginger
$\frac{1}{2}$ teaspoon cinnamon
$\frac{1}{2}$ teaspoon ground cloves
$\frac{2}{3}$ cup cake crumbs
$\frac{1}{4}$ cup shortening
$\frac{2}{3}$ cup granulated sugar
1 egg, beaten
$\frac{1}{3}$ cup molasses
2 tablespoons water

ORDERS: Sift flour, baking powder, baking soda, salt, and spices together. Add cake crumbs; mix well. Mix shortening and sugar; stir until light and fluffy. Add beaten egg and molasses gradually, mixing well after each addition. Add flour mixture and water alternately, mixing well after each addition. Drop spoonfuls onto greased baking pans. Bake in moderate oven (350°) 10 to 12 minutes. Remove from pans at once.

SLANG

Fish Eyes
(Navy; contemporary):
Tapioca pudding

QUEEN PUDDING
KOREAN WAR

One of the benefits of garrison duty was the chow. It was a lot better than eating cold beans out of a can while sitting in a ditch. (Come to think of it, there are a whole lot of things that are better than that.)

This isn't a recipe that would have been served in the field. And it probably wasn't served all that often on base either. This is a "special occasion" dish that combines fruit and meringue and all kinds of wonderful things.

FOR AN ARMY OF 100

RATIONS:
- 1 quart wheat cereal, uncooked
- 9 No. 1 cans evaporated milk
- 4 quarts water (for milk)
- 2 tablespoons salt
- 1 $\frac{1}{2}$ quarts granulated sugar
- 12 egg yolks
- 5 tablespoons lemon rind
- 1 No. 10 can, or 13 pounds fresh, fruit

FOR MERINGUE
- 12 egg whites
- 1 quart granulated sugar

FOR AN ARMY OF 10

RATIONS:
- $\frac{1}{3}$ cup wheat cereal, uncooked
- 1 $\frac{1}{2}$ cups evaporated milk
- 1 $\frac{1}{2}$ cups water
- $\frac{1}{2}$ teaspoon salt
- $\frac{2}{3}$ cup granulated sugar
- 2 egg yolks
- 1 $\frac{1}{2}$ teaspoons lemon rind
- 1 $\frac{1}{2}$ cups canned or 1 $\frac{1}{3}$ pounds fresh fruit

FOR MERINGUE
- 2 egg whites
- 1/3 cup granulated sugar

ORDERS: Add wheat cereal gradually to scalded milk, salt, and sugar. Cook, stirring constantly, until mixture is thick. Add a small amount of hot wheat cereal to beaten egg yolk. Return to saucepan and cook until eggs begin to thicken (about 3 minutes). Add grated lemon peel. Pour into greased pan. Cool until surface is set. Spread with well-drained, cooked fruit, berries, sliced fresh peaches or apricots. Top with meringue and bake in a fast oven (450°) for 6–7 minutes or until meringue is brown. Serve warm or cold.

To prepare meringue: Beat egg whites until stiff but not dry. Add sugar gradually; continue beating until light and the meringue stands in peaks. Add flavoring if desired.

SLANG

Gedunk
(Navy; World War II): Ice cream. More specifically, the table with the fixin's that you would put on top (syrup, nuts, cherries, etc.). The term is usually used in the phrase "gedunk bar."

VINEGAR PIE
WORLD WAR I

At the turn of the twentieth century, fresh fruit wasn't nearly as available as it is today. Refrigeration was rudimentary at best, and you needed to wait until a fruit was in season before you could get it.

Vinegar pie was a common result. Adding vinegar made a creamy filling with a sweet, tangy taste. When the military cook couldn't get fresh fruit, he could always get vinegar. For that reason, the recipe was included in the *Manual for Army Cooks* in 1916.

FOR AN ARMY OF 60

RATIONS: 5 pints water
$\frac{1}{2}$ pint vinegar
2 $\frac{1}{2}$ pounds sugar
6 eggs
10 ounces cornstarch

FOR AN ARMY OF 6

RATIONS: 1 $\frac{1}{2}$ cups water
1 $\frac{1}{2}$ tablespoons vinegar
$\frac{1}{2}$ cup sugar
1 egg
1 ounce cornstarch

ORDERS: Mix water, vinegar, and sugar and bring to a boil on range. Dissolve cornstarch in 1/3 cup cold water; then beat the eggs, adding them to the cornstarch and water. Add the whole to the boiling mixture on range. Stir well with a wire whip. Cook about 3 minutes and remove from range. There should be sufficient hot water added to the boiling mixture to make 1 gallon (1 1/2 cups). Piecrust must be filled while mixture is hot.

There's one in every outfit. Get a group of doughboys to pose nicely for a picture with their New York dressed turkeys and you can bet there will always be at least one guy who has to cut up for the camera.

ACKNOWLEDGMENTS

The pot that produced this book had but two chefs and we do take full responsibility for any errors or omissions. But the ingredients we used came from a variety of gardens and we wish to acknowledge those who provided the nutrients.

First of all, we are grateful for the comments, suggestions, and moral support we received from our editors and art directors, particularly Stuart A.P. Murray, Aaron R. Murray, Edwin Kuo, Rachel Maloney, and Glenn E. Novak. Sean Moore and Karen Prince, as senior executives of Hydra Publishing deserve our thanks for coffee and encouragement. Both were often sorely needed.

Donna Sanzone, our executive editor at Collins Reference, was a beacon of light during one or two dark nights (at least, those are the only ones she knows about). Thanks also to editor Lisa Hacken of Collins Reference for all her good work. Ellen Nanney is Senior Brand Manager with Smithsonian Business Ventures. She provided us with a generous supply of straws, at which we grasped with regularity and gratitude. Thanks to Jennifer L. Jones, David Miller, and the staff of the Smithsonian Institution's National Museum of American History, Behring Center, and to their exhibit: The Price of Freedom: Americans at War.

And we owe a great debt to Luther Hanson of the U.S. Army's Quartermaster Museum at Fort Lee, Virginia. His official title is Museum Specialist, but he will forever be known to us as a deep well from which we were able to draw historical fact, trivia, and lore. He pointed us in the right direction on several fronts, and we are grateful.

Finally, we wish to thank the men and women who have labored, for more than two hundred years now, to concoct the formulas that have fed the American military. If their efforts are ever acknowledged, it is often with derision. But not so from this quarter. At times creative, and almost never dull, the recipes they've promulgated have been the fuel that's powered the machine guarding our liberties. We are grateful.

We have made every effort to contact original copyright holders for appropriate permissions to reprint the images in this volume. However, several publishers are no longer in business, or could not be located. If rights have devolved to other entities, we encourage them to contact us.

—J.G.L. & P.J.H.

BIBLIOGRAPHY

MILITARY PUBLICATIONS

Department of the Air Force. *Technical Manual AFM-146-3, Recipes.* Washington, DC: Government Printing Office, 1950.

——. *Technical Manual AFM 146-11, Pastry Baking.* Washington, DC: Government Printing Office, 1966.

Department of the Army. *Technical Manual TM-10-405, The Army Cook.* Washington, DC: Government Printing Office, 1942.

——. *Technical Manual TM-10-405, Army Mess Operations.* Washington, DC: Government Printing Office, 1967.

——. *Technical Manual TM-10-411, Pastry Baking.* Washington, DC: Government Printing Office, 1966.

——. *Technical Manual TM-10-412, Recipes.* Washington, DC: Government Printing Office, 1950.

——. *Technical Manual TM-10-412-7, Recipes, Appetizers, Beverages and Soups.* Washington, DC: Government Printing Office, 1962.

Department of the Navy. Bureau of Supplies and Accounts. *The Cookbook of the United States Navy, NAVSANDA Publication No. 7.* Washington, DC: Government Printing Office, 1944.

War Department. *Handbook of Subsistence Stores.* Washington, DC: Government Printing Office, 1896.

——. *How to Feed an Army.* Washington, DC: Government Printing Office, 1901.

——. *Manual for Army Cooks.* Washington, DC: Government Printing Office, 1916.

——. *Technical Manual TM-10-410, The Army Baker.* Washington, DC: Government Printing Office, 1942.

BOOKS

The Charlie Ration Cookbook, or, No Food Is Too Good for the Man Up Front. Avery Island, LA: McIlhenny Co., 1986.

Commager, Henry Steele, ed. *The Blue and the Gray: The Story of the Civil War as Told by the Participants.* Indianapolis: Bobbs-Merrill, 1950.

Dickson, Paul. *War Slang: American Fighting Words and Phrases from the Civil War to the Gulf War.* New York: Pocket Books, 1994.

Dierks, Jack Cameron. *A Leap to Arms: The Cuban Campaign of 1898.* Philadelphia: J.B. Lippincott, 1970.

Dunnigan, James F., and Nofi, Albert A. *Dirty Little Secrets of World War II: Military Information No One Told You About the Greatest, Most Terrible War in History.* New York: William Morrow, 1994.

Farrow, Edward S. *Mountain Scouting: A Handbook for Officers and Soldiers on the Frontier.* Norman: University of Oklahoma Press, 2000. Reprint of 1881 edition published in New York.

Johnson, Clint. *Civil War Blunders.* Winston-Salem, NC: John F. Blair, 1997.

Kohn, George C. *Encyclopedia of American Scandal.* New York: Facts on File, 1989.

Musicant, Ivan. *Empire by Default: The Spanish American War and the Dawn of the American Century.* New York: Henry Holt, 1998.

Rose, Sergeant-Major Edward D. *Khaki Komedy.* Chicago: Howell Publishing Co., 1918.

Wooster, Robert. *Civil War 100.* Secaucus, NJ: Citadel Press, Carol Publishing Group, 1998.

Wright, Mike. *What They Didn't Teach You About World War II.* Novato, CA: Presidio Press, 2000

WEB SITES

Department of Defense. U.S. Army Quartermaster Museum, Fort Lee, VA: http://www.qmmuseum.lee.army.mil/

National Association of Civilian Conservation Corps Alumni: http//www.cccalumni.org

Naval Supply Systems Command. Naval Logistics Library Recipe Repository: http://nll1.ahf.nmci.navy.mil/recipe

PICTURE CREDITS

PHOTOGRAPHS: Division of Military History and Diplomacy, National Museum of American History, Behring Center, Price of Freedom Exhibit, Smithsonian Institution (negative numbers in brackets): 20 [2004-56149], 28 [2004-22517.09], 40 [2004-50204], 60 [2004-47030], 79 [2004-51185], 145 [2004-51837]. Guilford Courthouse National Military Park: 11. Courtesy of KF Holdings: 27. Kismet images: 8, 19, 34, 37, 49, 50, 63, 70, 88 (all), 114, 117 (both), 124, 128, 134. Library of Congress: 9, 35, 105 (Brady Civil War Photograph Collection, Timothy H. O'Sullivan), 113 (Works Projects Administration Poster Collection), 150, 163, 177. Military Museum of Gettysburg, Pennsylvania: 18. Morristown National Historic Park: 146, 155. National Archives: 86. National Park Service: vii. Photos.com: 121. U.S. Army: 4, 10, 53, 58, 76, 94 (U.S. Signal Corps), 102, 115 (John F. Kennedy Special Warfare Museum), 158, 172. U.S. Department of Defense: 3, 38, 41, 56–57 (U.S. Marines), 71, 75 (U.S. Marines), 81, 87 (U.S. Marines), 96, 108, 110, 119, 160, 168. U.S. National Archives: ii, viii, 46, 82, 107, 109, 111, 120. U.S. Navy: 6, 32, 78, 101. U.S. Quartermaster Corps Museum, Fort Lee, Virginia: v, 5, 97, 130, 162, 170. West Virginia State Archives: vi.

ILLUSTRATION: Rachel Maloney.